Bride's Guide to Emotional Survival

RITA BIGEL-CASHER, C.S.W., Ph.D.

PRIMA PUBLISHING

PRIMA PUBLISHING and colophon are trademarks of Prima Communications, Inc.

Library of Congress Cataloging-in-Publication Data

Bigel-Casher, Rita.
  Bride's guide to emotional survival / Rita Bigel-Casher.
    p.   cm.
  Includes bibliographical references
  ISBN 0-7615-0296-3
  ISBN 0-7615-1156-3
    1. Married women—United States—Psychology.   2. Wedding etiquette—United States.   3. Marriage—United States—Psychological Aspects.
4. Communication in marriage—United States.   I. Title.
HQ 1206.B39   1995
306.81—dc20   95-20683
                                               CIP

99 00 01 AA 10 9 8 7 6 5 4 3
Printed in the United States of America

HOW TO ORDER

Single copies may be ordered from Prima Publishing, P.O. Box 1260 BK, Rocklin, CA 95677; telephone (916) 632-4400. Quantity discounts are also available. On your letterhead, include information concerning the intended use of the books and the number of books you wish to purchase.

For HARVEY CASHER,
my extraordinary partner AND playmate:
for lessons in honesty, patience, and integrity.
For years of never-ending support and nurturance,
not to mention countless hours of invaluable editorial advice
and kitchen duty.

ONTENTS

One

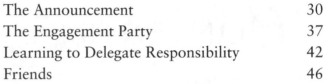

WEDDING POLITICS

PAIR-BONDING POTENTIAL

COMMUNICATION— IT'S A FAMILY AFFAIR

Five

HAMMERING OUT THE DETAILS   105

Six

MOTHERS AND DAUGHTERS   145

Seven

YOUR SECOND TIME AROUND   165

Eight

Nine

Ten

ACKNOWLEDGMENTS

To my treasure, my daughter Deborah Anne Bigel for cheering me on from start to finish, for her generous gift of reading many different versions of this book, and for teaching me about unconditional love and acceptance.

With love and deep affection to my dear son Daniel Bigel for his generous spirit and loving nature. I am very proud of the man he has become—an individual with integrity, strength, and the courage to be true to himself.

I am deeply grateful to my wonderful son Jordan Bigel for his invaluable assistance with suggestions to this book, but most especially for extensive and unstinting hours of nearly perfect patience with computer counsel, without which this book would never have been written.

Many thanks to my wonderful editor, Georgia Hughes, who was enthusiastically supportive and instrumental in helping me to get this work into print and into the marketplace way beyond her call of duty. I also appreciate the fastidious editing of Betsy Towner and the careful work of others on the staff of Prima Publishing. It's a pleasure to be associated with such an exceptional publisher.

I am blessed with an extraordinary group of family and friends who have critiqued my work in its various stages and given lavishly of their time with loving feedback and support. My love and thanks to my fabulous daughter-in-law Kate. And to Suzanne Grant, Laura Singer Magdoff, Elizabeth Kraft Jones, Carol Turturro Mehl, Robert and Shelly Schachat, my cousin Ruth Slakter, Evelyn Stupel, Judith and Steven Haveson, Emily Koltnow, Myron Pulier, Lila Nachtigall, Sandra Ramirez and Michael Araiz.

To all my wonderful teachers, and especially to these outstanding ones:

Richard Belson, my first mentor who gave me the initial delicious taste for Family Therapy and his invaluable professional and personal friendship; Gerda Shulman, a talented loving teacher who opened my novice heart to systems and family thinking; Jahmshed Morenas, my guru from Philadelphia Child Guidance who encouraged me to toss out my intellect and be true to myself as a clinician and a person. Elizabeth Carter, role model extraordinaire who gave me the valuable gifts of Bowenian thinking, feminist family therapy, and a healthy outlook on love and life; Steve Gilligan, the wondrous wizard who still helps me find my warriors, excavate my queen and king, get in touch with my hero, and bring to life my own magician.

In my private practice I work with remarkable people. I have learned as much from them as from my very best teachers. Effective therapy is a joint effort between individuals who respect and care for each other. I am proud that these are the men and women who have chosen me as their therapist, and very grateful for the contributions they have made to my book.

For thirty years I have been doing research, reading, observing, and learning from among hundreds of professionals in the social sciences. A bibliography that reflects some of my preferred choices is included. Considering the existence of the massive body of knowledge that is freely shared by all of us in the mental health field, there is a tendency for much of it to become blurred, as to original source. It becomes impossible to determine which scholar was the original contributor or even which unique source is being cited. My apologies if I have left anyone out. My book is the result of all the wisdom that I have collected from my own and others' experiences. I have tried to be watchful and incorporate references wherever a particular text is cited, though sometimes it has been difficult to recall the primary source, since this has all become my own way of thinking about how people live, love, and change.

In loving memory to my parents, Bob and Friedl Wolf.

Rita Bigel-Casher

$\mathcal{I}$NTRODUCTION

$\mathcal{M}$any women empathize when I compare the road to love and marriage to a ride on a merry-go-round. One moment you can be on top of the world, while the next you are on the way back down again. Just like the carousel, our romantic lives provide endless opportunities for excitement and joy. And one day, when horse and rider are in perfect sync, you and your true love grab the shiny brass ring and make a pact to marry.

So the journey to your wedding day begins. With a simple "yes," you set into motion one of the most emotionally charged and psychologically challenging of all society's rituals. Marriage, like birth and death, eclipses the routine of our daily lives through its sheer drama, symbolism, and importance. Expectations and sensitivities run high; your romance is thrust into the public spotlight. Add to that the complications of planning such an extravaganza, and the effect can be overwhelming. It's not surprising that more than half of all engaged couples experience very real pre-wedding stress that puts their relationship to the test.

This book was written to help you minimize and cope with the stress that often accompanies the pre-wedding process. This book really is different! Instead of dealing with the minutiae of choosing caterers, florists, and invitations, we will focus instead on managing the emotional hot spots that flare up as a couple plans their nuptials.

A secret that few brides share, perhaps because they think they are alone in their angst, is that they are overwhelmed by the onslaught of issues that crop up just before their wedding. Many lose their footing as they plot the many details of walking down the aisle. During this supposedly happy time, some couples find themselves squabbling and stressed out. Most soon-to-be brides find themselves dealing with at least one or two of the following issues: family pressures, money, differing religions and traditions, nerves, fear, second thoughts, and divided loyalty.

Any problem regarding one's wedding day is a nice problem to have, you might say. I totally agree. Weddings are magical and every bride is truly beautiful. The hidden side of weddings, however, can be an emotional roller coaster.

Getting married changes the family structure, which in turn can introduce tension for every family member. Questions of cooperation and separation come into play. Parental issues loom largest. The wedding arrangements become the field of battle where sides are taken and the love nest is sometimes in danger of being torn apart. Most family issues center around differences, and there are plenty—from who pays for what, to how many guests are allowed, to who throws the engagement party. Get ready to learn how to protect your relationship, don't get in the middle between your parents, and if the arrows are flying, learn to duck!

Most women fantasize that their engagement will be fun and glamorous. They discover instead that organizing a wedding is virtually a full-time job. Expectations and pressures run high, and couples who are unaware of this are often bewildered. Amid the frenetic wedding planning, one or both partners may begin feeling distant, moody, or confused. This confusion is sometimes compounded by basic gender differences in the approach to wedding preparations. Differing opinions regarding prenuptial contracts, responsibility, loyalty, and the complications of relatives and friends can add to the pandemonium. The ever-increasing duration of the American engagement can put a strain on any relationship. How do you cope with the infinite planning, the seemingly endless financial outlays, and the decreased frequency of intimacy, free time, and privacy? What if as the wedding date approaches, you find yourself (like many people do) experiencing cold feet, transient sexual dysfunction, and other assorted jitters? Am I doing the right thing? Is this person the one? Am I ready for this? Such anxieties are a normal part of the process of getting married and this book will help you deal with them.

Bride's Guide to Emotional Survival will teach you how to lead yourself and your partner through these issues in a way that preserves the integrity of your relationship and assists you in moving forward in concert toward your wedding day. This book combines meaningful information with important tools to enable you to combat all these difficulties and more. We will explore the underlying dynamics of pre-wedding stress and provide specific solutions to these problems.

Odds are that you will not need to deal with all of the issues discussed in this book. However, you can be assured that you will find an answer to your most common concerns regarding this important phase in your life. As you read you can also feel comforted to learn how other women have overcome similar or even more challenging problems.

Bride's Guide to Emotional Survival is about how to successfully survive those little surprises that could otherwise mar your wedding day. Throughout the book we will be exploring the elements of a healthy relationship to ensure that your marriage gets off on the right foot.

In my twenty years of experience as a New York City marriage and family therapist, I have been witness to a number of marriage proposals that actually took place in my office. I have been privy to the surprise and near-shock experienced by most affianced women as they were required to negotiate their way through the engagement phase. I have guided hundreds of women as they undertook the momentous task of making wedding arrangements. Their headaches and heartaches included getting past all sorts of potential pitfalls on the way to the altar. But by understanding the "what, when, where, and how" of a problem, we were able to devise solutions to overcome these pressing issues.

Becoming engaged and married can be a lot trickier than it sounds (isn't everything?). It's funny, because until we attain it, marriage is our goal. As we actually approach it, it becomes our obsession. And once we have it, it becomes our challenge.

You will meet a number of real people who have successfully conquered this challenge (names and identities have been altered to preserve confidentiality). You'll read about Rose, who had to stand up to her controlling parents in order to marry Bob. I will introduce you to Julie and Tim, who were blissfully in love until their marriage unearthed typical relationship issues. You will hear about Maureen, whose parents disapproved of her marriage to a man of a different ethnic background. And you'll learn how Lorraine dealt with her cold feet at the thought of living out her life with just one man, forever. Their stories are scattered throughout the book, giving you living examples of the dos and don'ts of successful, healthy connections.

The tactics in this book, along with your own good sense of course, will help you to achieve a joyful wedding and guide you toward a happy, satisfying life with your groom's loving arms around you.

CONGRATULATIONS, YOU DID IT!

Daisy, Daisy, give me your answer, do! I'm half crazy, all for the love of you. It won't be a stylish marriage, I can't afford a carriage. But you'll look sweet upon the seat of a bicycle built for two.
HARRY DACRE

*W*ithin weeks after they met Ellen knew she wanted to marry Greg. He was everything she ever wanted in a man. One year to the day after their first date, Greg proposed to Ellen. They were sitting on Greg's couch on a Sunday morning reading magazines and listening to the top 40 countdown on the radio. Suddenly, Ellen looked up from her *Cosmo* because she heard the DJ's special dedication from someone named Greg to someone named Ellen asking her to marry him. When Ellen looked over at Greg to see his reaction to this amazing coincidence, Greg was down on one knee at her feet with a ring in his hand and a smile from ear to ear. Needless to say, Ellen was stunned as Greg took her hand and asked her to be his wife. Ellen's eyes filled with tears and she fell into Greg's arms saying, "Yes, yes, yes, I would be honored to marry you."

*S*teve held out the ring as they bicycled their way through Alaska. And Judy, bleary-eyed from that day's 65-mile ride, fainted and fell off her bike. As Steve cradled her, the revived Judy stared at

the fourth finger on her left hand and beamed. A sweaty embrace, kisses, and tears were followed by the decision to get married with a minimum of fuss.

You're in love. You're engaged! You've said it, with or without words. It is on the table now—your relationship is "official." A marriage proposal launches a barrage of excitement, planning, and activity, all of which are also potential sources of stress. Certainly you expect a windfall of good feelings and want your wedding day to be picture perfect. But perhaps it is too much to expect that your engagement will be one nonstop party. Already you're realizing that there's a lot to deal with and your engaged and married friends are hinting that there are headaches ahead. Could all this frenzy have started with just one little question: Will you marry me?

It is probable that you, the soon-to-be bride, are now reeling from pre-wedding stress. This very real and common state results from the relentless wedding issues that have taken up residence in your life. Let's examine them one by one and try to make some sense out of the situation.

Of course you want to become married and live happily ever after. This is the goal of most men and women, and the goal of all parents for their children. It is also an objective that our culture and the media fosters. And no wonder, since it is such a pivotal part of the traditional family developmental cycle. Families in every culture throughout the world commemorate the significance of marriage, birth, and death. Let's face it, the ritual of the engagement, wedding ceremony, and reception are where it all begins.

Getting married is a major life cycle event. We are born, we become educated, we reach adulthood, we choose a profession, we marry, we have children, they marry, we care for our elderly parents, they die, we deal with old age, we die. These are life's turning points that punctuate everyday events, lending them extra weight. In all cultures around the world, these events are commemorated with ritual.

Rituals are ceremonies that enable us to pass from one psychological state to another and that are specific to a particular life event. They can be steeped in religious beliefs or myths or be secular. They are usually repetitive in content, action, and form. Rituals require some procedure that has a beginning, middle, and end. They evoke a certain mood as the drama is enacted.

Rituals have a social meaning and usually require one or more witnesses. The entire wedding process is a wonderful example of how rituals have been employed in our society.

Engagement marks the initial step toward this tumultuous tribal ritual. You would think it should be a period of happiness marking your transition from a beloved child to a loving and responsible adult. Yet, as ecstatic as you may be to embark upon the official road to marriage and adulthood, reality is beginning to dawn. There is another side to weddings: Along with great happiness there is also turmoil during the engagement and pre-wedding period. Why? Because this time represents a significant transition from childhood to adulthood and a great upheaval in numerous areas of your life. It is only a myth that engagement is a time of pure bliss for the prospective bride and groom. What you really end up experiencing is a large dose of joy, a dash of ambivalence, and a healthy helping of stress.

On television and in the movies, planning a wedding looks exciting, glamorous, and fun. Blushing brides try on gorgeous gowns. Happy grooms are fitted for tails, plan honeymoons, and attend bachelor parties. An endless parade of caterers, floral designers, musicians, and wedding gifts flows through the house. It is hectic but elegant and civilized.

In real life, planning a wedding doesn't usually proceed as smoothly. There are a multitude of decisions, unrealistic expectations, sensitive subjects, and concerns along the way—any one of which can be a potential booby trap. Given the strain, people may get cranky and even downright cantankerous. Animosity can erupt between couples who periodically need to remind themselves that they are madly in love.

Sure, this is the happiest time of your life and you're having the best time. Yet it also feels as if you are in a pressure cooker, a disaster waiting to happen. You don't have to let yourself get thrown by the mixed emotions and stressful experiences common to this post-engagement phase. Let's make one thing clear—organizing a wedding is virtually a full-time job. Chances are that no one (except your girlfriend who got married last month) can understand why you are so busy, least of all your partner.

With the announcement of your engagement an endless roster of questions, decisions, appointments, opinions, complications, constraints, and compromises accumulates. No wonder people elope! When one woman I know broke the news of her engagement to her parents, her father congratulated her and then said jokingly, "Honey, if you want, we'll get you the best ladder money can buy." When faced with the headaches of planning a wedding, eloping in the middle of the night seems an attractive alternative. Don't be surprised if you entertain this thought. Do persevere, however. It is worth it!

Lengthy engagements further complicate an already complex situation. Stretching out to a year and a half, two years, three years, and beyond, long engagements are becoming the norm in a culture captivated by the image of wedding day "perfection." Try booking a location for the reception or getting a bridal gown in less than six months and you will discover that the wedding industry calls all the shots. Yes, I did say wedding "industry." Just flip through one of those five-pound bridal magazines or rent the movies *Father of the Bride* or *Betsy's Wedding* and you will see what I mean.

It is easy to become caught up in all the fuss and commercialism as you plan your wedding day, especially with all the outside pressures from family, friends, caterers, and wedding consultants. But if you can stay focused on the fact that this is *your* celebration marking your special transit in the normal family life progression, you'll come a lot closer to your ideal wedding.

If you are like most of the women I meet during the course of my work as a marriage and family therapist, you may have mistakenly believed that the task of finding the "right guy" was the only hard part. But now that you are faced with planning your wedding, you are doubtless discovering that the hard part may lie ahead. In fact, you and your fiancé are probably asking yourselves, "Who needs this?" And your parents, in-laws, stepparents and siblings feel the strain, too. It is no wonder. Organizing a wedding is intricate. Getting to the altar takes a small miracle. In fact, many describe the final experience as simply a huge relief.

Finding pleasure on the road to marriage requires a basic awareness of the psychological process of weddings. What is really going on here? Isn't this just a party, albeit a grand one? Why is it so difficult? One of the reasons for pre-wedding stress is that planning your special day is a new and unfamiliar experience for every family member, even if you are not your family's first offspring to leave the nest, and even if you have been married before. For you and your fiancé, planning the wedding begins your life together as a real partnership.

On another level you also may be experiencing some discomfort regarding the large step you are taking. This is quite normal. After all, getting married is shouting to the world, "This is the one and only person I love and intend to be with for the rest of my life!" It can be a frightening concept. What an enormous leap of courage and faith—in oneself, in each other, and in the institution of marriage. As if that's not enough to deal with, here comes the clan!

Let's start by exploring two concepts relevant to the early engagement phase: Family Life Progression and Marriage Readiness.

THE FAMILY LIFE PROGRESSION

Learning about this concept is very useful, as it provides the foundation from which to understand the emotional dynamics underlying the formation of anxiety between "Yes" and "I do." When you have a clear awareness of *why* upsetting things can happen, you gain a new perspective. This knowledge helps you deal more effectively with a troubled episode, your feelings, and your family.

Getting married is an act of confidence and maturity that leads to further emotional growth. If this is not your first time, you have presumably learned a lot already. Whatever your previous experiences, you are now embarking on a new path. (Chapter 7 deals with stress unique to remarriage.) Every prospective bride is altered both personally and as a member of her "family of origin" (in other words, the parents or stepparents who raised you and your siblings).

There are a multitude of factors rooted in the changing structure of the family that induce tension. Stress comes from two different sources: It can be either self-induced or generated when you are reacting to someone else who is feeling tension. Radical modifications in family membership—such as "losing" a daughter and "gaining" a son—resurrect old issues, which frequently exhibit themselves in conflicts regarding the wedding celebration. Unresolved problems between family members, buried for years, may erupt as well. If your parents are divorced (Chapter 4 explores such issues in greater depth), be especially watchful for fiery responses. Times of upheaval shake up the family order and neglected issues, like old relatives, often resurface.

Each child has a special meaning to each parent, and each plays a vital, unique role in the family. When a child marries, her or his role is permanently vacated, resulting in an emptiness. The resulting void is experienced by each family member in a different way, depending on the role the marrying child played for that family member.

The internal emotional struggle that surrounds the approaching emptiness is expressed in one of two ways. It can be addressed directly by means of personal acknowledgment and through conversation, or indirectly through the conflicts surrounding the various aspects of planning the wedding. Such feelings of loss are manifested in arguments and disagreements about details regarding expenditure of money, inclusion or exclusion of specific family members or friends in the wedding party, and the many issues of control that necessarily arise during this time. If family members would only consider this emptiness as the true source of their battles, they could choose to stop their aimless and destructive bickering. By honestly sharing fears and anxieties, the underlying sensitivity and caring can return, putting the real issues in perspective.

Evelyn was ready to call off her wedding and elope when she and her fiancé, Bill, came to my office. Her parents were dictating their preferences, threatening to cut off their funding, and creating daily tension that affected every other aspect of Evelyn's life. "I think we should elope," said Bill, who was quite upset by his fiancée's tears as she told the stories that overshadowed this supposedly happy time.

In exploring the family picture with Evelyn, we learned that as the only daughter she held a special position in her mother's life—the two women were exceedingly close. Upon further investigation,

Evelyn realized that she was the only person her mother had ever had a long-term, intimate relationship with—Evelyn's parents had a rather distant marriage. Evelyn's grandmother had died in childbirth to her only child and Evelyn's mother was subsequently raised by a maiden aunt. The aunt died when Evelyn's mother was twelve and she was then cared for by her grandfather until his death a mere four years later.

Though Evelyn had always known these details of her mother's life, she had not recognized their impact. In the course of our work together we reasoned that the woman who was so controlling over her daughter's life was probably compensating for her feelings of fear connected with the upcoming loss of her adored child. Furthermore, once married, the connection between the two women would have to change. Evelyn's mother had no way of knowing in advance exactly what form the change would take, which must have caused her enormous anxiety.

Bill suggested, "Evelyn, I really feel bad for your mom. Maybe I should talk to her so she could be assured that I won't come between you."

"No thanks," said Evelyn, sniffling again, "I think I should be the one to talk to her. She must be so at sea about all this, and I want to tell her how much I love her and how I will always need our friendship." In fact, after Evelyn and her mother had that conversation, everything regarding the wedding seemed to settle down to a manageable level. The mother of the bride was indeed reassured and cried happy tears as her daughter walked down the aisle.

STEPS IN THE FAMILY
LIFE PROGRESSION

1. Young adults become
   emotionally and finan-
   cially independent
   from their family of
   origin.
2. They find partners, fall
   in love, marry, and
   switch their loyalty
   from their original
   families to each other,
   forming a new family.
3. They have their first
   child.
4. Their first child goes
   off to kindergarten.
5. Their children reach
   adolescence.
6. Their last child goes
   off to college.
7. The couple learns to
   deal with the empty

   (continues)

Evelyn's willingness to put her anger aside momentarily while she looked beneath her mother's impossible behavior allowed her to rectify a very difficult situation for herself, her partner, and her mother.

Getting married is a big change for you and your family. Steps in the Family Life Progression trigger intense emotions among family members. Families pass through predictable developmental stages, each of which contains an inherent loss or gain of a family member, each of which holds the potential for crisis as the family regroups, as well as opportunities for creative change. There are roughly twelve stages.

Each stage in the Family Life Progression, including the process of getting married, is inherently defined as a crisis. Change creates upheaval regardless of whether the alteration is positive or negative or whether a family member is gained or lost. Each person in the family experiences large measures of stress, confusion, and emotional upset during any life cycle change and the group as a whole needs to accommodate itself to the new configuration.

Getting married is the most stressful phase in the family developmental cycle because you are involved in *two* family life changes at the same time. You are in *stage two,* finding a partner, falling in love, marrying, switching loyalty from original families to each other, and forming a new family. On the other hand, your family as a whole is in *stage nine*, children get married and leave the family. Given that this is a double delight makes matters just a little bit more complex. Not surprisingly, the process of getting to the altar can sometimes feel like a feud between the Hatfields and the McCoys.

Getting married is also a highly defined rite of passage, and conflicts between the engaged couple and their parents are a crucial aspect of the transition. Although extraordinarily uncomfortable and disquieting, the fighting is a necessary phase in the process of separation. It ensures that the couple advances emotionally from their roles as children to adults establishing a new family. This core of pre-wedding stress is rarely revealed. Our culture, the media, and the family classify this event as a festivity—which of course it is— and ignore the enormous adjustments that accompany engagement and marriage. Whenever a stage of the Family Life Progression is successfully negotiated, the next step will evolve more naturally and easily.

If you have already developed a sense of emotional and financial independence—as was your task during the first stage of the family developmental cycle—then

nest and with e
other again.

8. The couple confronts middle age, menopause, career changes, dealing with their aging and dying parents, and planning for retirement.

9. Children get married and leave the family.

10. The first grandchild is born.

11. The couple deals with retirement, old age, and financial changes.

12. Each person deals with his or her own and mate's death, related illnesses, or disabilities.

the process of getting married will contain minimal up-heaval. What is required of you in the second stage is to switch your primary loyalty to your soon-to-be husband and to establish yourselves as a couple. What often happens is that one does not entirely complete the task of growing up, and getting married provides a second opportunity to do so.

The various issues that circulate throughout the wedding planning period—right up to and including the wedding day—are vehicles through which this final transition from childhood to adulthood is carried. Pre-wedding stress may be an indication of leftover work from the first stage in the life progression. If the second stage, getting married, is not successfully worked out, then it is quite likely that the third stage, having a baby, could bring with it stressful components that will threaten the marriage. At that point there will be a further opportunity to complete emotional tasks from previous stages. And so it goes.

When wedding conflicts do occur, be reassured that the family is at least dealing with the work of separating, instead of sweeping it under the rug. It is unusual for a couple to have achieved complete independence from their families prior to their wedding. Such a rare occurrence would allow the family to simply celebrate

15

...ings better by taking the following steps. Begin by stopping your reactivity for a moment and ask yourself what might be motivating that person to be so difficult. Is it possible that he or she is feeling threatened by the possibility of losing you? Is he or she feeling left out of your life? Try to deduce

(continues)

their wedding day as the symbol of the new couple's change in status. What is helpful to remember is that the conflicts being stirred up during this pre-wedding period are a significant aspect of emotional growth and are ultimately beneficial. Think of this time as a second chance to complete the process of growing up. For you, the bride-to-be, the entire wedding planning phase is a wonderful opportunity to ensure future happiness. Consider each conflict with your family as a precious moment that you can harness to confirm your status as an adult and to establish your bond as a couple.

several possible reasons for his or her behavior, taking into account that person's own family history and patterns of interaction with others. Once you have become sensitive to that person's motivation you can approach him or her in a reassuring and loving manner. Your conversation can open up previously unknown areas of intimacy, improving your relationship in general and furthering your ability to enjoy a beautiful wedding day.

"*T*his was supposed to be the happiest time of my life," cried Laura during one of her therapy sessions three weeks after announcing her engagement to both sets of family. "I'm feeling torn apart," she continued. "My parents want me to have a traditional all-out kind of affair, while Barry insists on a low-key, small wedding."

"Laura , what do you want?" I countered.

"I'm not sure," she responded and was then silent for a time. "I think I'd like a small informal wedding, too, but then I'd feel like I'm taking sides against my parents. They've always done so much for me. They'll feel hurt."

I suggested, "It is natural to feel a conflict of loyalty at this point in your life. Who do you think needs to be number one in your life?"

Unhesitatingly, Laura responded, "Well, Barry is going to be my husband. I guess I do have to take his side, especially since I agree with him."

"So what's next?" I asked.

"I guess I ought to tell my parents and get ready for battle."

Much to her surprise, Laura discovered that the fur did not fly and that her parents were quite willing to compromise, once aware of her and Barry's wishes. Taking a stand alongside her fiancé was an important statement about their relationship. It drew the couple together and, in a sense, placed a safe boundary around them. For Laura, it meant that she was able to satisfy both herself and her future spouse. Even more importantly, her willingness to assert herself with her parents underlined her readiness to be a grown-up. It takes two adults to make a healthy marriage.

As you move through each stage of the Family Life Progression, you will be called upon to make crucial relationship changes. Your willingness to satisfy your own needs and take responsibility for yourself allows you to complete the first stage in the cycle. This naturally includes your ability to withstand your family's disapproval. And making your future husband number one in your life is at the crux of fulfilling your task during the second stage.

MARRIAGE READINESS

In the previous section, Laura's willingness to express what she did and did not want signaled her completion of the first stage in the Family Life Progression. This indicated her level of emotional maturity and *marriage readiness,* a term I devised to describe an interesting concept.

Remember when you were in grammar school and your teacher referred to your state of "learning readiness"? This was defined as the degree to which your reading, writing, and social skills were age-appropriate. It determined if you would be promoted to the next grade. A similar definition can be applied to marriage readiness: Are you emotionally and developmentally ready to move out of your role as someone's daughter or son and become someone else's spouse? Your marriage readiness level predicts how well you interact with others, your likelihood of success in finding a marriage partner, and whether you will make your marriage a happy one.

IDENTIFY, ACKNOWLEDGE, ASSERT

- *Identify:* Look inside to determine what you want.
- *Acknowledge:* Pretend to be in your parents' shoes for a moment to gain their perspective on the subject.
- *Assert:* Be willing to tell your parents the truth about your feelings. Stand up together to your respective families and politely assert your wishes.

The fact that you have gotten engaged and are planning your wedding is a pretty good indication of a fairly high level of marriage readiness. In other words, you are in the process of disengaging from your childhood role as your parents' child and engaging in your adult role of becoming a spouse. We can see how Laura, in order to make this transition, accomplished her difficult task by doing three things: identify, acknowledge, and assert.

First, Laura needed to *identify* what she herself wanted. Second, Laura needed to *acknowledge* her parents' feelings—show them she understood their point of view. Third, Laura had to find the courage to *assert* her status as a soon-to-be wife to Barry. Like so many other things in life, the fearful anticipation of a thing is often greater than its reality. The wedding planning process contains a multitude of opportunities to alter your childhood role and to become the adult that you are.

WHOSE WEDDING IS THIS ANYWAY?

With reasonable parents you can enjoy comfort in expressing and following through with your wishes regarding your wedding. Such parents become your partners in your effort to let go of your childhood. In fact, growing up is ideally a joint process between parents and children, where children pull toward independence and adulthood and parents push for separation and growth.

Unhappily, you may have parents who are tenacious in their need to hold onto you. To express that need they make unrelenting efforts to control every situation. Their motivation to hold onto you emanates from the emotional baggage they carry and *not* because you are incapable of taking on adult tasks. Your obligation to yourself and to your future spouse is still the same. You must decide what you want and don't want, and find a calm, friendly, and respectful attitude with which to express those inclinations.

In a worst case scenario, be prepared for your parents' difficulty in accepting the fact that you are an adult with your own ideas who deserves to have her wishes respected. Keep in mind that the conflict with your parents is a necessary step in your journey toward your wedding day. Prepare yourself to acknowledge your parents' feelings and to counter any negative responses with calm declarations. At worst, they'll disapprove or temporarily reject you. As an adult you can survive others' disapproval. It is not pleasant, but certainly possible.

*R*ose encountered a most difficult situation when she and Bob decided to hold off on planning their wedding for several months while they took time to acclimate to their new status. The young couple announced their engagement and their decision to their respective parents. Rose's parents disregarded their daughter's resolution, booked their country club and caterer for the following June, and then ecstatically informed the young couple of the done deed.

Bob and Rose came to see me because of the nightmare that arose between them and her parents. Rose's parents said it was too late to cancel anything because of the down payment they had already made. Bob threatened to cancel the engagement unless Rose stood up to her parents and stopped them from taking over their lives. Rose felt scared about the consequences of taking the necessary stand with her parents. She expected they would probably stop talking to her, since throughout her childhood this had always been her parents' way of punishing her when she disagreed with them.

Fortunately, Rose took Bob's upset seriously and used this as an opportunity to practice taking an adult position with her parents for the first time. We outlined some statements that she could make to her parents, as well as probable rebuttals from them and counter responses from her.

Rose's parents were as angry and unforgiving as she had anticipated. They refused to speak to her for several months. During that time Rose contacted them regularly, just to touch base. This was designed to show them that she was committed to her decision, but not willing to let go of her relationship with her family. This was a highly stressful time for Rose. Her commitment to her own growth and to the well-being of her upcoming marriage kept her going.

Eventually her parents came around. Something wonderful happened in the course of this process; the parents of the bride learned to respect their daughter in a totally new way. Their relationship flourished. Six months later, the wedding took place without a hitch.

The alternative to asserting yourself is not pretty. Sooner or later your marriage will suffer if you do not take these steps toward separating from your parents. Be sure to share your experiences with your fiancé because the same, of course, is true for him. He must renegotiate his relationships with his family, and sometimes he will need your encouragement and support to bring this about. Certainly none of these potential obstacles should stop a couple from having the wedding of their dreams.

Each member of the family has a unique set of apprehensions. Your parents have their own concerns and worries: How will this change my relationship with my son? Can my daughter do better? What is this going to cost me? How will we cope with an empty nest? Have I been a good mother? Your siblings may experience a variety of feelings as well: How come my younger sister is getting married before me? How will my brother's marriage change our close friendship? Can I learn to

Women who still see themselves principally as a daughter cannot be free to become a wife. If they marry they will not succeed in creating a healthy marriage unless they throw off the shackles of dependence on their parents.

love this stranger who is taking my sister away from me? Will they ask me to be in the wedding party?

At the same time, your anxieties may focus on: How will this change my life? Am I giving up my independence? Can we afford the kind of wedding we truly want? Does my sister always have to control things? Can't my parents get along even now? How will I ever get organized? What role is my stepparent supposed to play? Do I really want this? Is my life over or just beginning? What if I don't get along with my new in-laws? Do I have any say at all? Am I supposed to be thinking like this? Help!!!

Most weddings do not take place without at least a tiny family-related calamity. Sometimes close friends present unexpected problems surrounding issues of choosing members of your wedding party and seating arrangements (see Chapter 2). My hope is not to scare you, but rather to help you anticipate the worst possible scenario. In this way your ability to withstand disaster will improve since it will not take you by surprise. Just being aware of the issues that concern others can help you to be more relaxed as you deal with them.

For example, you don't have to take your divorced sister's attitude personally when she acts uncooperatively while selecting a gown. You can guess that her anger may spring from her internal conflict about her own life and try to be sympathetic to the difficult time she must be having. Putting your arms around her and lovingly asking, "Sis, what can I do to help?" can ease a difficult moment.

Once you can put yourself in someone else's place, no matter what part they play in the marriage drama, your ability to deal with them is enhanced. When your parents bicker about the menu, you might notice how each may be fighting for your attention, and lovingly settle the matter instead of just getting annoyed. You might also note that your parents may be suffering the loss of your loyalty when you take your fiancé's side in an argument. This is as it should be, yet their feelings are valid, they are real. Reassuring your parents that you love them, but that your partner needs to be your first priority, would probably be met with acquiescence and understanding.

What if this isn't so? What if your parents appear to be too needy or too self-absorbed to open their hearts and minds to your point of view? What if you find yourself crying in your fiancé's arms every night as you recount to him (or listen to his) formidable family stories? Couples who confront just this sort of situation can feel completely lost.

FAMILY
SURVIVAL KIT

1. Allow yourself to fully experience your sad, mad feelings toward your parents. You are normal to have an intense emotional response. Give yourself the freedom to luxuriate in your upset.

2. Here is a step-by-step approach to enable you to get through the difficult process of enduring the pain of hurt or anger. You don't have to deny these emotions.

   a. Find a quiet, safe, and private place.

   b. Think about the incident that triggered your pain. It may be useful to write it down in detail.

   (continues)

Remind yourself to be satisfied that you are doing everything possible to create an amiable climate, and that your family has to do their part to adjust to your upcoming status as someone else's wife, and not just their daughter. Do the best you can and then brace yourself to withstand your discomfort should it arise. Your parents may just need more time and in the interim may be uncooperative. Soothe yourself by supporting and reassuring yourself that ultimately you can only do so much. Find comfort in your partner as you find strength in your unity.

Think about it this way, it was a matter of luck that determined the family you were born into. Good, bad, or indifferent, you were dealt a hand. You are stuck with your family, but how you play your hand can make all the difference between winning or losing. If you have the unfortunate luck to be in a difficult family, the Family Survival Kit may contain some helpful pointers for you to consider.

The ultimate goal is for you to have a wonderful time preparing for your wedding and pulling it off. Recognize that it is inevitable for at least one or two issues to surface and that when conflict strikes you may feel resentment, frustration, and anger. Try to remember that despite their fussing and fighting, deep down each and every family member wishes you and the man you love the utmost happiness. At the same time, all are involved in the difficult crisis of adjusting to the new family condition. So with a little patience and determination you and your partner can arrive at the altar with all your relationships safe, well, and happy.

SURVIVAL TACTICS

You probably have an image of your wedding day—and I am sure it differs from that of your parents, let alone your in-laws. Money disputes, conflicting tastes, jealousy, and loyalty issues can also add to your headaches. You'll need to learn to walk skillfully around this minefield so that you'll emerge alive and well and living in happy matrimony.

Your mother and father have, in all likelihood, experienced pressures for you to get married as a way of solidifying their self-image as good parents. These conventional pressures give credence to the belief that only through marriage can their offspring experience happiness and success. They very likely feel that once you have walked down the aisle, they will have "graduated" their child. But whereas your father had always wanted you to get married, it is probably your mother who has

c. Locate the site in your body where you sense the pain physically. Close your eyes and actually feel the anguish.

d. Other thoughts, memories, and emotions may occur to you. Now that you are an adult you can be open to that past experience and heal your past and present hurt.

3. You may cry or feel like screaming. Give yourself permission to express the entire range of your emotional self. (Repeat this process as often as you need to until you feel better.)

4. Once you have taken time to be alone with

(continues)

your agitation, share these experiences with your fiancé. Start off by asking him to just listen. Ask him to withhold any advice or suggestions for the time being—he doesn't have to fix anything but simply attend to what you are expressing. This will bring you closer to each other. (You might wish to repeat this process several times.)

5. Now you and your fiancé can put your heads together and list some options for handling the situation with your family. Decide what course of action would bring you the greatest sense of satisfaction.

thought about your wedding nearly as much as you have and may even have squirreled away a nest egg for that event. In some instances your parents will also have definite ideas about your wedding, including specific plans for your gala.

And then there are those parents who want you to have a beautiful wedding for their own personal gratification—these might be the take-over type of parents who leave you little room to express your individual preferences. Some parents have a need to express their success as a social statement and their adult child's wedding is an opportunity to build their self-esteem by showing off with extended family members or friends. Regardless of the type parents you have, it is quite likely that you, not they, will make the lion's share of the decisions regarding your wedding.

Your parents will be an important part of the festivities, of course, and you'll want to find ways to cope with their idiosyncrasies. Planning a wedding brings out the best and the worst in people—especially parents. From the ceremony to the cocktail napkins, most parents experience a burning desire to get involved in every last detail of their child's wedding and to have their opinion count for something.

To both your parents, the wedding drives home the fact that their baby has grown up. It seems as if it was only yesterday that they swaddled and cooed at their new bundle of joy. Could it be that so many years have passed? They are probably marveling that you are old enough to be getting married—it makes them realize how quickly the time has passed since they taught you how to walk and talk and since they saw you off to your first day of kindergarten. That was their first letting go and it wasn't easy. They were concerned about whether you would like school, how you would get along with the other children, if you would be a good student. They probably recall the fierce independence or the fear you exhibited about going off by yourself—or your insistence about choosing your own school outfit.

Through the years there were many more separations, many more steps up the ladder of maturity and in the Family Life Progression. Yet each succeeding movement toward adulthood did nothing to change their attitude—you were still their child. When you were hurting, they were the ones you turned to. Even when you came back from college and you all felt like strangers, there were those moments of special closeness. When you obtained your first promotion they were the first ones you called. And they really thought they were losing you for good when you moved into your own apartment, but then you asked your parents to help you decorate and, perhaps, for a loan. And whenever they came to visit, they sort of felt at home puttering around your kitchen or watching TV. But now all that has changed! Their baby is totally grown up! And you belong to a new family system. They will no longer be the first to soothe you, to smooth the rough spots, to share that special knowing smile. Your husband will be!

WEDDING POLITICS

The joys of parents
are secret, and so
are their griefs and
fears.

FRANCIS BACON

How long do you keep the good news to yourself? Whom do you tell first? You have just made a decision that will change the course of your entire life and you may need a little time to absorb it—that is quite natural. Many couples prefer it that way. Up until now you have been totally involved in the romance of your relationship. As such, it has been a private situation between you and your partner.

Now, however, your impending marriage brings your commitment into the public sector and your relationship becomes an official linking of two families. Marriage is a social contract—an "institution" in the legal, religious, and political sense that sustains our cultural system. As such, it transcends the pure relational aspect of the natural pairing process that you have experienced thus far. Depending on the sensitivity levels

involved, you may wish to establish certain priorities before you go ahead and publicize the fact of your engagement.

THE ANNOUNCEMENT

Dealing with the formal announcement is the first step in joining yourself and your family with your partner and his family. Get ready for potential family fireworks. For example, there may be trouble ahead regarding who is told first, second, or last. Such complexities will be the major focus of this chapter. We will also discuss how to manage your engagement party, should you decide to have one. In addition, we will explore how to deal with your respective families when it comes to handling others' input, needs, and preferences regarding your wedding day.

When Jack and Amy decided to get engaged, Amy could not wait to share the exciting news and called her mother the same evening. Jack, on the other hand, did not feel the rush. This is what they told me during our initial conversation.

Jack recalled, "A couple of weeks later we flew to Chicago to visit my father and stepmother, a plan Dad and I spontaneously hatched during one of our rare telephone conversations. Dad and his wife were thrilled when we told them our news, but all hell broke loose a few days later when Mom learned that I'd told Dad before telling her."

Amy said, "I felt so bad for Jack—he didn't mean anything by it. His Mom really came down hard on him, crying, and telling him he was an ingrate after all she'd done raising him all by herself."

Jack responded, "It wasn't such a big deal . . . I really messed up . . . I'm pissed off at myself for hurting her like that. But you know, I can't believe she's still competing with Dad—doesn't she know I love her? Maybe I'll talk to her again when she calms down."

Jack and Amy had not considered the impact that getting engaged would have on the family. Old divorce skeletons emerged from Jack's family crypt in the form of competition between his parents for his love. Whom he told first was defined by his mother as an indication of whom he loved best. The situation was probably unavoidable, yet Jack's upsetting feelings could have been minimized had he assumed the Boy Scout stance, "Expect the worst and be prepared!"

Having divorced parents (or any family members who are cut off from each other) adds an additional burden. These people whom you love don't love each other—they may even be archenemies. Sure, it is unfair

Dear Mom,

I am writing to you in the hopes of clearing the air between us. First, I want you to know that I love you very much and the last thing I would ever want to do is hurt you in any way. You have been such a great mom to me, a guy couldn't have asked for better. When Dad walked out on us you were stuck with a little kid, me, and you could have walked out on me, too, but you didn't. I know how hard it was to raise a son by yourself, and I know that sometimes I gave you a hard time. We got through all those tough spots and you raised a good person—if I say so myself. *Thank you!*

(continues)

that you have this extra layer of responsibility, but since you are stuck with this situation, you may as well learn to be effective in negotiating the field between your parents. (See Chapter 4 for more about divorced parents.)

It's beneficial to be sympathetic to your parents' sensitive feelings at this time of family transition. So, whenever possible, before you take an action that involves one of them, ask yourself what the other's reaction might be. You don't always have to take your parents' feelings into account when you make decisions. But it would be of enormous benefit to you personally to be able to predict all aspects of your decisions. Who knows? You might even take a more political position so that a future upset is avoided.

Be that as it may, Jack did not have this foresight and had to deal with his mother after the fact. What he did was write a letter to pave the way for a personal conversation. Letters are a wonderful therapeutic tool. You as the sender can take your time to communicate your feelings in a relaxed fashion, choose your words carefully, edit endlessly, all without the anxiety that face-to-face contact can sometimes hold. The receiver, on the other hand, has time to digest your statement and avoid the emotional reactivity that sensitive subjects often elicit.

Word spreads quickly among the ranks of family and friends. Once the shock and excitement of the announcement is assimilated, you enter the new and very complex arena of wedding planning. This is why I advise newly engaged couples to take a few hours (or days!) to themselves before announcing the news. I call this time the "calm before the storm." Specifically, I think it makes sense to have a discussion with your fiancé and agree on a few basic things before you make that first phone call. These basics can include the approximate wedding date and the ring. Everyone will ask, so you want to be equipped with this minimal information. Some couples leap into gear and are fully armed with their wedding vision before going public. Others foolishly believe that engagements can be free of wedding talk.

Eve and Peter thought they could get away with it. He surprised her with a ring a mere five months into their relationship. Eve was initially reluctant to accept Peter's proposal considering the brevity of their relationship. But he and their friends convinced her to consider a long engagement. Eve relented and truly believed that she and Peter would continue to advance their romance since their wedding date was a full year away.

Once the news was out, their families got in gear. Eve found herself propelled into action. After all, the best church and caterer

So what happened? I'll tell you, Mom, I didn't mean to hurt you. Dad asked me to come visit and that was right after Amy and I decided to get married, and it just didn't seem important to make a big deal.

Dad finding out first is in no way an indication that he is more important to me than you are. Please don't believe that for one minute. I guess getting married is a big production and old issues come out of the closet. I want you to know that Amy and I want you to be a big part of our wedding. I'll call you next week so we can plan when to get all of us together.

Your loving son,
Jack

had to be booked a year in advance, and how can those decisions be made without determining the number of guests, let alone the type of affair? Before she could say *abracadabra*, Eve's life became immersed in wedding details.

But Eve need not have worried. There were plenty of opportunities for growth. With each turn of events the arrangements created fertile ground for the couple to move their relationship forward. Eve quickly got to know the intricacies of her fiancé's relationship with his parents, his attitude toward money, and his love for her. She made a point to spend quality time with Peter devoid of wedding talk and insisted that some of the time the couple spent with friends and family be devoted to just having fun.

In the above example, Eve and Peter found that wedding plans inserted themselves into their everyday lives prematurely. It was unrealistic to believe that their relationship would not change once it entered the public domain. Many couples opt for a very long engagement that affords them time to get accustomed to each other and to handle wedding details at leisure. Others complete fundamental wedding business quickly and put the rest aside until they are closer to the wedding. Remember, this is your wedding and you can manage it in whatever way is best for you and your relationship. If nosy relatives pressure you for certain details that are as yet undecided, you can always politely refuse to be pushed.

In any case, once engaged you will be inundated by suggestions from family and friends. Do you have to listen to uninvited advice? No! You are an adult. Even though it is rude to offer unsolicited advice, well-intentioned relatives are hard to stop. You don't need to take them too seriously as they bombard you with instructions. Just let things roll over you. You are not obliged to answer any questions unless you want to—"I don't know yet" is an acceptable response. This means that you do not have to compromise yourself. Try to keep maximum peace and harmony during the flurry of family input. And you might as well accept that everyone will be forthcoming with novel ideas and preferences right up until the day of your wedding.

Now that they know of your engagement and have probably grilled you with a million questions, what are some appropriate guidelines for you, your parents, and your fiancé's parents to follow? No doubt they will be eager to get involved and it would be so nice if you could, to some degree, allow that. Considering the impact of your engagement on the entire family, your

> **ANTIDOTE TO PUSHY RELATIVES**
> One helpful way to save your psyche is to do what one woman I know did: Create a suggestion book. Purchase a small spiral notebook and whenever anyone offers a pointer, smile sweetly, pull out your pad, write down the idea, and thank them very kindly. The advice-giver will experience pleasure that you are taking them so seriously. Who knows? One day when you are leafing through the notebook you might just be inspired by one of them.

wedding, in the strictest sense, is a family affair. Everyone involved is beginning the difficult process of integrating the news.

Ideally, the two sets of parents (or sometimes three or four sets if there have been divorces in your families of origin) initially should do nothing more than act as public relations agents. Wedding finances, religious issues, guest lists, and catering arrangements can wait, although often they do not. Chances are pretty good that all these details began churning in your parents' minds the moment you sprang the news. Hold them off! The folks should be encouraged to work the phones, happily spreading the good news far and wide. In this way they can perform a valuable service (you didn't really want to call his Aunt Tilly in Toledo, did you?) while giving you some breathing room. After all, parents wait their whole lives for a child's wedding day, and they will be bursting with pride as a flurry of questions comes your way.

Daughter: Hi, Mom! Please get Dad on the phone. Joe and I have some good news.

Dad: We're both here. What's up guys?

Daughter: We wanted you to be the first to know. Joe and I are getting married.

Mom: Congratulations, I'm so excited! So when's the wedding? Where? Here or in Boston? Can I call everyone, or do you want to?

Dad: Molly, give the kids a minute to catch their breath. Joe, Karen, we couldn't be happier for you. And Joe, welcome to our family.

THE ENGAGEMENT PARTY

And so it all begins! If you have decided on your wedding date you may now be considering an engagement party. There are no rules regarding the how, when, what, or where of this celebration—it is a matter of what you, your fiancé, and your families want. Whether you decide on a small intimate party at your parents' home or a huge blowout at your local country club, you are bound to encounter some interesting complexities. The challenges presented will be forerunners to the ones that will probably emerge at your wedding. Think of this as an opportunity to practice.

Let me tell you how Lisa fared when Jeff surprised her with a ring for Christmas.

*T*he wedding was set for the fall and within a month of the announcement, Lisa's mother mentioned her desire to throw a small party in her apartment. She proposed to invite a few of her friends who had known Lisa since childhood, Jeff's immediate family, and the couple's close friends. Lisa and Jeff loved the idea and Lisa's mother contacted Jeff's parents to ask about available dates in February.

Lisa's parents had been divorced since she was in high school and like many formerly married couples had an antagonistic relationship. This of course had always been difficult for Lisa, who loved both of her parents and despite their animosity enjoyed a healthy relationship with each of them. The way Lisa's parents had operated over the last ten years was to ignore each other. This had worked quite well because there was truly no need for them to communicate; their daughter was an adult and could negotiate her relationships with her parents independently. The engagement, however, raised new issues. For one thing, Lisa wanted her mother to invite her father to the engagement party.

When Lisa raised this issue, her mother initially resisted the idea, saying, "But I'm giving you the party in my home and it has nothing to do with your father. After the way he treated me, I can't believe you could ask me for such a thing!"

Needless to say, Lisa was very upset. She needed to find a way to approach her mother in order to gain her cooperation so that her father would be included in an event that he had a right to attend. But first she needed a game plan. The steps listed below were very helpful to Lisa and resulted in a positive outcome. If you have a heated issue that you need to resolve with someone, try them yourself.

Game Plan for a Difficult Issue

1. Make an appointment to spend some time alone.
2. Choose a neutral place to meet, such as a restaurant or a park.
3. It is not necessary to tell the person in advance what the topic of your meeting is if you are afraid that they might not be willing to talk about it.
4. Prior to the meeting make some notes about the points you want to discuss. All too often one can become anxious and forget important details.
5. Prepare yourself for the meeting by assuming the worst possible outcome resulting from your conversation. Perhaps write out some of these possibilities or talk them over with someone. Also, list some negative responses and think about how you will deal with them. Decide what position you plan to take should you fail to reach an agreement.

6. Just prior to your meeting do something comforting and relaxing so that you are in a positive frame of mind.

7. Begin your meeting by initially spending a little time in superficial, friendly chitchat. This sets up a pleasant atmosphere.

8. When you feel ready to begin your conversation, ask for the time to just be listened to without interruption. Reassure the person you are addressing that they will get equal time to respond when you are done. Wait to get their agreement on this style of conversation before you proceed.

9. Present your points in a calm, pleasant, and respectful manner—keep your voice modulated. Make your points as short and clear as possible. Spell out what your concerns are, what you want from that person, and if applicable, what you are willing to do as well.

10. If at any time during your presentation you are interrupted, do not respond to the interruption, but rather ask the person to continue waiting for you to finish. (You may have to do this more than once.)

11. When you have finished, stop and be quiet.

12. Carefully listen to the response that you get. You might be surprised to learn how that person feels and it may actually have an impact on your initial thoughts on the subject. Do not interrupt.

13. If you are met with antagonism, disapproval, disagreement, or a lack of cooperation, be sure to validate the person's feelings before you continue. For instance, you can say, "I understand this is what you believe," or "So, according to what you feel . . ."

14. Now it is time to pull out the big guns and to state your position should your desires be obstructed. Once again it is important to present this idea in a friendly, neutral way, e.g., "I must tell you that I feel very strongly about what I am asking for and if you don't see your way clear to going along with my needs then I will have to . . ."

15. Then you may need to repeat certain points again. Be sure to do so in a calm manner and be careful not to become reactive to the anxiety that might be elicited. (The last two steps may have to be repeated.)

16. If you get no cooperation during this meeting, you might encourage the other person to take some

time to reconsider the points you have raised and promise to call them in a few days to talk things over again.

17. When you take your leave, be sure to do so in a neutral manner. Whatever happens, do not succumb to an angry attitude.

Lisa was very pleased about the outcome of her conversation with her mother. The bottom line was that she was willing to tell her mother that she would forgo the engagement party if her father was not invited. This was not something she truly wanted, but Lisa felt that she had no choice, that it would have been wrong to exclude her father.

When Lisa's mother understood Lisa's strong feelings, she agreed to write her former husband a note and invite him to the party as her guest. The party was a great success.

LEARNING TO DELEGATE RESPONSIBILITY

Chances are you will be planning your wedding day with your mother and possibly even include your stepmother or future mother-in-law in the preparation process. Some combination of the female family group

generally becomes the main moving force in getting
things done, a state of affairs which is typical in most
cultures, where women are in charge of the marital rite
of passage.

Men often take a lesser role in mapping out the festivities, though they are usually involved financially.
However, since your wedding affects everyone on both
sides of the family, their sensitivities ought to be considered. Ideally, your role will be that of a good manager
who encourages her assistants to take responsibility for
the hundreds of details that need to be dealt with,
including researching for places, caterers, music, and
photographers. Everyone feels validated when they are
consulted, and if you anticipate that, as manager of this
joyous enterprise, you will usually be met with cheerful
cooperation.

Unless you are a perfectionist, you can have a wonderful time as you allow others to be part of the planning. A bride who is a perfectionist falls into the trap of
believing that no one can do as good a job as she can, or
that if her wedding isn't perfect her guests will be critical. The good news is that your guests are far too
involved with their own agendas—what to wear, who
will be there, and who will baby-sit their kids—to give
much thought to anything but having a great time at

your wedding. Your fiancé probably doesn't share your concern for perfection either. All he knows is that he loves you, wants to spend the rest of his life with you, and if the wedding is too much of an ordeal in the making, he'd just as soon forget it and elope—unless he's a perfectionist, too.

Perfectionism can spoil your fun and everyone else's. It can especially get in the way of your most important goal: uniting harmoniously with your partner. Preparing for your wedding provides many opportunities to build healthy relationship skills that you'll be able to use throughout your upcoming marriage. Believe it or not, the issues that crop up will seem irrelevant when compared to the problems you'll need to address once you have children. Please note that the solid foundation you build together now will cushion your future family life and provide the invaluable team structure that a healthy family depends upon.

Typically, the things that lead to fights, hurt feelings, and scenes during the engagement phase are separate situations that have been brewing for a long time. The precursors of trouble are issues that you and your partner have not settled with each other or with your individual families. In particular, if either of you is overly involved with them, it could lead to wedding-related stress.

Perhaps you and your mother have some unresolved issues between you—for example, you didn't get along before you got engaged or undercurrents of hostility or hurt have not been discussed or rectified. Other sources of conflict can result from heightened sensitivity during this time if your mother is deceased or if your stepmother raised you (more about this in Chapter 6). These formerly unspoken difficulties may emerge at this time.

Tension between yourself and any family member will interfere with making this special time in your life as wonderful as it should be. A smart bride follows the adage that "an ounce of prevention is worth a pound of cure" and ferrets out potential trouble spots even though they are barely perceptible. Creative Conflict Resolution presents a simple three-step formula you may want to refer to again and again concerning any issue with a family member or friend. Give some thought to potential trouble spots. Ask yourself, "Which person in my family might get especially stressed, obnoxious, or difficult?" or "What situation related to my wedding might give rise to someone in the family getting upset or getting me upset?" or "If someone were to create trouble at my wedding, who might that be?"

It would be helpful if you share some of the exercises presented in this book with your fiancé. Let him in on

CREATIVE CONFLICT
RESOLUTION

1. Go through these steps
   with each trouble-spot
   person you have identified. Begin by deciding
   who will be the easiest
   to approach. Find pri-
   vate time to talk with
   her or him. The goal
   for your talk is to use
   "I" language (nonac-
   cusatory words that
   simply state what "you
   yourself" feel or want)
   and to make a state-
   ment that clearly and
   in a friendly tone ex-
   presses your concern
   and your ultimate goal.
   It may be helpful to
   write it down before
   your talk. For example:

   "Mom, I wanted to
   talk to you because
   I'm a little worried.

   (continues)

what you are discovering and how you are handling things. Then, ask if he would like to go through the same steps in order to ward off potential problems in *his* family.

FRIENDS

Even your friends—who have always been your saviors in helping you deal with your family—may require special attention during this time.

Mary Sue's wedding plans were nearly complete and everything was proceeding just as she had always wished. She and the man she adored decided to hold a small affair in nine months. Their parents were getting along and being extremely cooperative. The charming inn she coveted was available and they booked it. Yet she was in a frazzle.

Two things in particular created Mary Sue's pre-wedding stress. First, she had just lost one of her closest friends, who was devastated at not having been asked to be a bridesmaid. Second, her job was getting in the way of dealing with the ever-mounting wedding particulars that demanded her attention. To make matters worse, no one seemed to understand or care as much as she did.

After Mary Sue and I talked about her feelings of guilt and regret about her girlfriend, she came to realize something important: Weddings have a mysterious aura of significance for everyone involved that stimulates all sorts of unfamiliar reactions.

The bride-to-be has no option but to make choices that please her, her fiancé, and their families. And inevitably some people will disapprove, feel left out, or be insulted. Believe it or not, some friends may get annoyed with you for choosing to get married on their anniversaries or on holidays they consider to be inconvenient. Other friends may feel upset that you did not invite their children, their parents, or even their own best friends. Then there are the bridesmaids who aggravate over having to wear the color or style of dress you have chosen. Don't forget the impossibility of pleasing everyone.

Yet, these interpersonal breakdowns naturally create enormous anxiety. Mary Sue had to do the best she could with these painful situations. She could take the time to clarify her position with the friend who felt hurt, knowing that ultimately not everyone would be understanding.

Mary Sue wrote a letter to her girlfriend, Sara, explaining her rationale for assembling her small wedding party and expressing her sorrow at her friend's agitation. She pleaded with Sara to reconsider breaking off their relationship and emphasized how

Since you and I sometimes don't see things eye to eye, we might fight about how things will be done for my wedding. I want us to get along and I need you to tell me if something bothers you about the wedding plans. Please understand, however, that it won't necessarily mean that you will be able to do things your way, but rather that we will bring it out into the open and find a comfortable solution. So let's make a deal to talk about things as soon as they occur."

2. Then, just be quiet and listen.

3. If you are met with any kind of agitation, calmly repeat your statement.

much she cared for her friend. Mary Sue understood the possibility that Sara was an excessively sensitive person and that perhaps their friendship would have ended at some point anyway.

Mary Sue also came to terms with the necessity of finding functional ways to contain wedding business. She faced the fact that her job merited her nearly full attention while at work. She decided to relegate her lunch hours to making the dozens of pressing phone calls that steadily collected. In addition, Mary Sue enlisted the women in her life to deal with some of the crises that demanded attention. In fact, she realized that this was a way to both alleviate some of her stress and make her friends and family feel more a part of her important time.

Mary Sue also came to terms with the reality that only those who have encountered pre-wedding stress firsthand could truly comprehend her turmoil. The bride's role is much like that of the lone sheep dog whose diligent job is to keep the herd moving forward, bring back those who stray off course, and look out for predators.

PAIR-BONDING POTENTIAL

$\mathcal{T}$he engagement period, while intensely romantic for you and your partner, can also be a time of moodiness and confusion. You can expect certain changes in your relationship, including less or different sex, a loss of focus on everything but the wedding itself, and a feeling of grief and/or fear regarding the end of your single status. A long engagement period can be beneficial in that it gives each of you the time to work through these feelings and to establish your relationship as a solid pair. Emotionally, it is a complicated period for you both.

$\mathcal{K}$en was a lot like his father. Shy and soft-spoken, he had somehow fallen in love with Liz, a talkative, vivacious woman who always got her way. Liz had been pushing him quite vocally (after all, it was her style) toward marriage for two years. After a period of quiet reflection (that was Ken's style), he decided that he wanted the same thing, and the couple became engaged.

CHAPTER Three

When a man and woman decide their association should be solemnized and legalized with a marriage ceremony, they pose themselves a problem which will continue through the marriage: Now that they are married, are they staying together because they wish or because they must?

JAY HALEY

49

For two weeks after the announcement Ken was on cloud nine. Nothing could upset him, not even his friends' joking remarks that Liz had pushed him into getting married and that she would always wear the pants in the family.

For a while Ken went along with the flow of engagement parties, family meetings, and wedding planning. But soon he noticed that he and Liz never went out on dates or had much fun anymore. When they were together Liz talked endlessly about the wedding and was constantly on the phone making appointments. To Ken's dismay he was being asked to make dozens of decisions and was often the center of attention among family and friends, sometimes even having to speak publicly—all activities that made him anxious and went against his nature. Worst of all, their sex life had almost entirely dried up.

Ken was at the end of his rope until he spoke up to Liz during a rare respite. Liz took Ken's complaints seriously. She helped him to isolate the problems that bothered him the most, such as the loss of intimacy between them. Ken also revealed to his future bride that he dreaded even the thought of being put on the spot to speak in public. Once Ken experienced Liz as a true friend again, he was much relieved. Together they focused on, and resolved, one issue at a time. He felt more in control of the whole situation and was able to get on with the wedding agenda.

If your prospective groom seems rattled by wedding stress, pay attention. It is to your benefit to set aside wedding details periodically and remember to stoke the embers of your love. Ken is a good example of a highly involved groom-to-be. It is very possible that your fiancé may be like-minded and want to actively (even if reluctantly) participate in wedding procedures.

If you are fortunate enough to have a partner who is open and forthcoming with his feelings, he will let you know when he feels left out or uncomfortable. If, however, your man is less inclined to be direct, you may need to keep your antennae on the alert for signs of discomfort. It may be necessary for you to raise the topic yourself. Hopefully, as he experiences your willingness to listen to him, he'll learn to be more forthcoming with his upsets. But what if your partner seems to take no interest at all?

GENDER DIFFERENCES

Men and women are still very distinct despite our society's worthy determination to gain equity between the sexes. Let's hope for equality, but *viva la différence!* Aside from being raised differently, we have dissimilar styles of relating to the world. Men are biologically and psychologically driven outward toward action and goals. Women are more reflective and sensitive to their own and others' emotions.

Remember when you were five and played "Wedding"? Or when you saw your cousin Beth before the ceremony so beautiful in her seed pearls and lace? Or when you looked through the family photo album and saw the happiness in your parents' smiles on their wedding day? Odds are you dreamed about your own wedding and what it would be like. Women spend many years preparing for their special day, thinking and planning, so by the time a woman gets engaged she quickly propels into action. If you are like most soon-to-be brides you probably did something you swore you never would—you stopped at the nearest magazine stand and bought every bridal guide!

Family and culture have prepared women not only for their wedding day but for life thereafter, including the emotional closeness required to share life with another. Women have developed a natural propensity for marriage and intimacy. Girls are encouraged to talk to one another about feelings, as well as to express emotions. Society and family permit us to feel sad, to feel pain, and to cry. The sharing of these particulars leads to intimacy.

Our culture does not encourage boys to express such feelings, which are often labeled "weak." Men are more often permitted to express anger and aggression.

These are most definitely valid feelings, yet ones that create distance rather than closeness. Most girls derive pleasure from emotional closeness with their mothers and girlfriends. As adults they seek similar relationships with men. Girls naturally identify with their mothers, who are viewed as role models, and when they grow up, they seek to create a family of their own. In addition, a vigorous biological nesting drive urges women toward marriage. For the most part, women hope and expect to have wedded bliss and children.

On the other hand, men rarely think about their wedding day per se, though they do spend a great deal of time pondering the idea of getting married. Both men and women encounter an inordinate amount of pressure to become coupled, as if there is a stigma related to being unattached. Success as an adult in our society, in general, is still defined as the combination of happiness derived through work and love. Many people fear that others will view them as somehow deficient if not married.

Most individuals sigh with relief when they become engaged; the pressure is off, they are following tradition and are about to embark on the same journey as their parents and grandparents—hopefully with a greater degree of success. Of course, there is a little more to this

> A man looks pretty small at a wedding, with all those good women standing shoulder to shoulder, making sure that the knot's tied in a mighty public way.

as well. There is the personal joy of knowing you will be sharing your life with your soul mate. The wedding itself, however, is generally much more important to the bride than to the groom, which is often a point of contention between couples.

What do you do if you are feeling upset or angry with your fiancé because he is not getting involved in anything beyond the honeymoon? Some women have complained that their partners willingly follow "orders," yet do not initiate taking care of wedding chores. Interestingly, this is also a common lament among married women regarding housework and childcare. Perhaps both problems share a common basis, since men perceive planning a wedding as nothing more than making a party and therefore consign it to the domain of women.

In most cultures, women have taken charge of the wedding ritual. Historically, women have felt more comfortable with the organizing and entertainment aspects that a wedding party entails. Men tend to be left out, and believe it or not, many men prefer to adopt a low-key approach to wedding planning and many women honestly don't mind one bit.

Traditionally, our culture has divided responsibilities according to gender. Women have been trained to create a home and nurture its occupants while men have been relegated the role of economic provider and protector of the home. Originally, such selection had purpose when our ancestors lived in primitive circumstances that required physical strength to fend off attackers. Men and women were well-suited physiologically to fulfill their respective roles. Of course, these circumstances no longer apply. In these modern times, women and men usually share the financial burden and both are equally capable of participating in nurturing functions.

Given this historical baggage, however, couples today still struggle with defining their roles. The engagement period is the time to begin negotiating for the kind of relationship you want to have in the years to come. If you are satisfied with a traditional structure that assigns roles according to gender, then be prepared to be in charge of most things that are related to hearth and home—including wedding planning. If, however, you and your fiancé seek a more equitable approach to marriage, then new rules would apply.

WORKING TOGETHER

When a partnership is well-tuned, each member accepts responsibility for specific facets of the union. First and

A TYPICAL BRIDE
AND GROOM'S FALL
FROM GRACE

1. They fall in love.
2. He proposes or they decide to marry.
3. They decide to have a wedding.
4. She talks about the kind of wedding she's always dreamed of.
5. He loves her and wants her to be happy.
6. He goes along with what she wants and has few ideas of his own.
7. She is ecstatically designing her fantasy wedding.
8. He perceives the wedding as her territory and area of expertise.

(continues)

foremost you must agree on your mutual goals. In the case of weddings, what's required is that both you and your fiancé are in accord regarding the type of wedding planned. Once this is established, what will naturally occur next is a joint understanding of each partner's obligations as they apply to achieving the agreed upon goal. This could include clarifying the various duties that the couple needs to accomplish and the assignment of specific tasks. With mutually selected goals, the job of dividing chores should run smoothly.

The problem many women face, however, is that the wedding of their dreams is *not* in the image of what their fiancé values or desires. Men often agree to go along with their fiancée's wedding concept, albeit without accepting this as a shared goal. This then leads to misunderstanding between the pair.

What do you do if this scenario sounds familiar? You can learn something valuable about relationships. If you choose to fulfill a thing that is meaningful to you but not to your partner, be prepared to carry it out alone or with a minimum of collaboration. Nothing is wrong with this style of goal-setting. Let's face it, it's impossible to have joint agreement about everything. In the course of your relationship there will be many instances when something will be important to you but not to your partner, and vice versa. In such a case, you are responsible for bringing it about. If your partner is willing to help you reach your objective—great. But do not expect his enthusiasm to be equal to yours.

Though many women complain about their partner's lack of involvement during the engagement period, there are always exceptions. In some instances, women enjoy taking the backseat and men take on the lion's share of organizing their wedding.

Stuart was the one who took charge of the kitchen and home and was the creator of fanciful dinner parties that awestruck friends eagerly attended. When he and Dorothy decided to get married in his parents' backyard the following autumn, Stuart immediately went into gear. He was the one to call caterers, to decide on the menu, and to initiate talk regarding finances with their respective families.

Dorothy was quite happy to let Stuart control the situation. She was highly involved in her work as a computer programmer, had little interest in food, and didn't know the first thing about organizing a party. Frankly, it scared her. However, after a while she felt left out. When friends and relatives asked her about the details she'd say, "I'll check with Stuart. I'm not quite sure what we decided about music (or flowers or guest lists)."

While shopping for her wedding gown with her mother (her only wedding chore) she confided that she was a little unhappy with the present arrangement. "I feel sort of excluded from my own wedding," she told her mother.

9. She goes full speed ahead into the exciting fun of masterminding the big event.

10. Her whole life is focused on the wedding.

11. He goes on with the rest of his life and misses her emotional presence.

12. She becomes overwhelmed and exhausted.

13. He tries to be understanding and is willing to help her.

14. She gets angry and resentful that he is *helping* her when she wants him to *share* the responsibilities.

15. He is angry, resentful, and confused since he didn't want such a fuss in the first place.

GAINING YOUR PARTNER'S COOPERATION

1. Tell him you miss his participation.
2. Ask him if he would be willing to involve himself in some capacity, and if so, how would he enjoy contributing or in what area is he skilled in taking over (e.g., music, caterer, attendants' gifts)?
3. If he does not come forth immediately, help him to decide or let him know which chores you would like him to take on. If it is

(continues)

Dorothy's mother encouraged her to sit down with Stuart and tell him what she was feeling.

After talking with Stuart, Dorothy felt much more comfortable. She told Stuart she wished to take charge of the music, the writing of the vows, the selection of clergy, and the invitations. Stuart was most relieved to share the burden and they lived happily ever after.

However, if your fiancé is of the more traditional variety and seems disinterested in the planning process, ask yourself: Is he comfortable with the apathetic role of the groom-to-be? Maybe he is. Or perhaps he feels lost or overshadowed by all the excitement. You never know. Is he jealous of all the attention being paid to you, his bride? It happens! Does he feel like he was coerced into a big fancy affair? I have heard men say that. Or is he just following cultural expectations regarding men's lack of involvement with weddings? Most likely he just does not care very much about the minutiae involved in the wedding preparations—that which absolutely fascinates you leaves him somewhat bored. But until you communicate with your partner you are only guessing.

Often, however, when a prospective groom does give his input, his bride shoots him down. Since the majority of men are not especially savvy about weddings, sometimes women unintentionally help maintain the very situation they so ardently wish to change. No wonder! Women have also acceded to this controlling social role and sometimes perceive themselves as the experts in things related to hearth, home, and weddings. If you do want him to be more involved and are willing to step aside a little, try the approach in Gaining Your Partner's Cooperation.

In a large sense, the issues that occur during the engagement period are excellent preparation for marriage. Most women in our culture have been trained to take over household and emotionally related matters. A party, even one as grand as your wedding, is typically considered to be "woman's work." If you want your future husband to shoulder some of the household tasks in the years ahead, now is the time to begin.

Sometimes a groom who wants to be involved in the wedding plans is being left out of the decision-making process or steamrolled by the women in the family. Traditionally, the bride and her mother do the bulk of the work in preparation for the wedding. Remember to

important to you, you might insist he take on at least one chore.

4. If he chooses a task, notice your inner response. Do you feel relieved of some responsibility and pleased? (Good!) Or do you feel a surprising sense of discomfort and worry about whether he will be able to carry out his chosen task(s)? (That's good, too. At least you're aware of your ambivalence.)

5. Now comes the hard part: Sit back and let your groom-to-be carry out his responsibilities.

include others in the process, whether they be your fiancé or his mother or father.

A year after his wedding, Danny was still resentful that his family had been totally left out of the wedding preparations. He nurtured this resentment until it hardened into a stone wall between himself and his wife. The problem was that at the time of the wedding he never voiced his true feelings to his bride.

"Do you really think it's not too late?" asked Danny during one of our individual sessions. "I don't know if my parents will ever get over it," he continued. "Do you know, they still talk to me about their pain at having been so grossly disregarded. As for me, if I talk to Betsy about it now she'll be in shock. It's like we had two weddings. Hers was great. Mine was depressing."

"You are not responsible for Betsy's feelings," I answered. "For that matter, it might be useful for you to tell your parents to get over it. Your job is to communicate your feelings, thoughts, worries, and joys with your wife. Without honest conversation with Betsy your marriage will continue to suffer. It will be her job to deal with her own emotions in response to you. Besides," I assured Danny, "I have complete faith that you are both reasonable people. And even if Betsy becomes upset by your revelation, in time she will come to appreciate your courage to be truthful. Don't you think she wants your marriage to succeed?"

Something wonderful happened after our session. Danny realized that the most important thing was to fight for his life with his wife. Danny first told his parents that he no longer wanted to discuss the wedding with them. He explained that when they tried to ally with him by complaining about his wife, it created disharmony in his marriage. And after Betsy and Danny talked, he was gratified by her loving response.

It is appropriate and desirable for your fiancé to stand up to you, his soon-to-be bride, if he is feeling left out or if his wishes are being ignored. Unfortunately, many men are uncomfortable introducing potentially explosive subjects. They fear emotional confrontation and tend to give up their point of view in personal matters rather than argue for what they truly want. (Interestingly, these same men are often quite aggressive in business.) This is their problem *and* yours—theirs because they don't like rocking the boat too much and yours because you have to deal with them. If your partner is the silent type, he probably fears hurting you or getting hurt by your reaction to him. How do you encourage him to voice his feelings? Try the method described in Breaking Silent Patterns.

Some people think they are communicating effectively when, in fact, nothing of the kind is going on.

BREAKING SILENT
PATTERNS

1. Tell him that you
   would like to have a
   straightforward rela-
   tionship.
2. Ask him what you can
   say to elicit his can-
   dor.
3. Ask him what you do
   that may discourage
   his honesty.
4. Actively listen to him
   whenever he does
   express his opinion
   (which does not mean
   you must do what he
   wants).
5. Be careful not to dis-
   miss him or argue
   your point too often or
   too harshly. Make an
   attempt to tone down
   your manner when
   confronted.

Do not mistake a childish temper tantrum for an appropriate challenge to the status quo. A fair proportion of people let off steam when they feel stress. This is quite different from standing up to someone, which requires telling the truth about what you do or do not want in a reasonably mature manner. In other words, being assertive!

On the opposite end, do not be willing to accept too much acquiescence from your partner. Dare him to declare himself to you. Otherwise, you might end up in a marriage where you are in charge and resentful, while he is distant and resentful—not a good combination. The same methods apply if *you* are the silent one in your relationship. However you manage things, the key is for the two of you to communicate on issues as they arise, so that neither of you feels neglected or left out.

THE UNKNOWN FUTURE

In the midst of the frenetic activity surrounding the planning of your wedding, you may experience a feeling of disorientation—most brides do. It is really not surprising since you have just begun the process of attaching yourself to another. Every gain is coupled with a loss. Every loss is experienced as a death. When we gain our heart's soul mate, we lose something very real as well. We lose an aspect of our own identity as a separately functioning individual, as a child, as the daughter of our parents.

Of concern to many couples is the fear of losing independence. Marriage does not mean imprisonment. A good relationship is an interdependent one. This implies a healthy combination of dependence on one another and an independent attitude toward life. One of the things that makes a marriage truly great is creating a system where you feel both single and married. On the one hand, you can each experience tremendous satisfaction from your close friendship and the time that you spend together. At the same time, you both also have the freedom to attend to the things that are important to you as individuals, like work, friends, and hobbies.

Getting married means bringing together your life with that of another and making him or her the most important person in your life. It also means that your relationship with your partner receives star-billing and deserves the same kind of loving attention and concern as you give to yourself. No matter what, you should be his shining star and he yours! Nothing less will do.

The following illustration shows the structure of a healthy relationship. Two people (the circle is the female and the square is the male) who are each individuals connect and thereby create a third entity, their relationship.

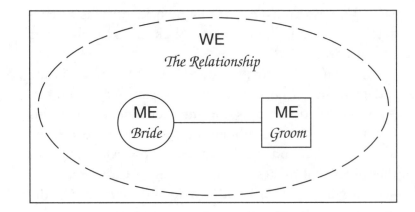

Each person in a well-tuned marriage is a "me" while also existing in the context of a "we."

A new relationship structure forms when you become engaged such that your obligation to yourself now includes an obligation to your relationship. To create a hearty marriage, each of you needs to commit to the growth and vitality of both yourself and your relationship. The way to accomplish this is to focus daily on actions that enhance the integrity of your relationship *and* yourself.

When two people decide to marry, they make a commitment, a sacrifice that is an emotional investment of time and energy in their relationship. That's what it means to make a pledge. The "we" becomes as great as the "me." True love exists when your partner's satisfaction or happiness becomes as significant as your own. Sometimes people believe that when two people marry, they become one. This is a dangerous idea, I think, because when one plus one equals one, some *one* got lost in the ceremony. There is a joke that goes like this: A woman says to her friend, "My husband is in charge of everything. He is the boss and I am nothing." Her friend responds, "If you are nothing, then he is the boss over nothing."

Coming to terms with a new lifestyle is never easy. It might be helpful to talk about this with your fiancé. The chances are quite good that he, too, is struggling with this issue. Talk about what each of you expects married life to be like. Perhaps you each can list the changes you expect to occur in your day-to-day existence concerning specific areas of your life such as work, friends, family, and money. Share your ideas with one another. If there are differences in your expectations (which would not be surprising considering you are two different people, a woman and a man raised in two different families), be ready to negotiate the points that might create future conflict.

THE CONSEQUENCES OF HONEST COMMUNICATION

1. You'll feel better just having shared your concerns.
2. You won't feel so alone with your upset.
3. You'll feel closer to your best friend in the whole world.
4. You'll learn something new about what you are feeling just by talking about it.
5. You'll learn something new about your partner.

(continues)

*G*ina and Scott were fast approaching their wedding day. All the decisions had been made. It seemed feasible that the engaged couple could be carefree and enjoy their last few weeks of courtship. But something was amiss.

Gina had not spent an evening alone with her friends for some time. Certainly she looked forward to her bachelorette party, and she always enjoyed Scott's company. But she missed the intimacies that she and her best friends used to share over dinner without men. She was afraid to exclude Scott because she thought it wrong to want this. After all, her parents never went out without each other. Her idea of being coupled was to be joined at the hip—and she didn't like it.

One day Gina took a risk.

"Scott," she tentatively began, "I was thinking of making plans with Marni, Danielle, Deborah, and Kate next Tuesday night. What do you think?"

"What a great idea!" Scott replied. "You know, I'm glad you took the first step," he continued. "I've been wanting to see Daniel and Jordan but have been reluctant to say so. I was afraid to hurt your feelings and make you feel left out. I feel so much better now." Scott put his arms around Gina and said, "I sure picked a great woman!"

Remember, your marriage does not have to be like anyone else's. You and your partner are free to create a unique arrangement that meets your particular needs of the moment, recognizing that these will change as your marriage progresses. Every couple has its own set of individual preferences and needs. Your marriage does not have to be like that of your parents, siblings, or friends. Most importantly, listen to your inner voice or intuition and talk to your partner. The Consequences of Honest Communication lists the possible outcomes that you can expect as a result of such a conversation.

Relationships can be difficult during the wedding planning phase. It helps to realize that there are often glitches that periodically obstruct the loving feelings, and that's just the way it is. I define a "glitch" as a seemingly irresolvable problem that pops up unexpectedly. It helps to be prepared for those little monsters and to keep in mind that when a glitch rears its ugly head it is not the end of the relationship. Instead, see it as a wonderful opportunity to learn something new about each other and to become more firmly connected once the disaster has passed.

Bear in mind that closeness is never a constant. Real life concerns, and wedding details in particular, can disrupt the harmony between you and your fiancé. Feeling incredibly close to your partner for a period of time and then creating some distance for a while is also natural.

6. You'll learn something new because your partner will have some feedback.
7. You'll put into place a healthy pattern of sharing that will enhance the quality of your marriage.
8. You'll realize the problem is bigger than you thought and will seek professional help for yourself and/or with your partner. Thousands of couples participate in some form of premarital counseling.

The purpose of this is to allow each of you to recharge your personal batteries—attend to your own needs and interests—and then become emotionally available to move closer again. This cycle is in constant motion.

It is comforting to know that each position—the closeness as well as the distance—has a vital purpose. What's more, it is kind of fun to enjoy the distance when it occurs, because it gives you the space to focus on yourself, your friends, and your own interests that are not part of your life with your fiancé. And of course, when the closeness returns it is absolutely delicious!

A mature relationship is a lot like an emotionally healthy person whose moods maintain a fairly steady rhythm of ordinary ups and downs—sometimes feeling a bit better than others. The following illustration shows this cycle. Just like the people in it, the mood of a healthy relationship also fluctuates along a similar continuum. Sometimes you are close, sometimes distant. Passion increases and decreases from time to time—especially while you are planning your wedding.

This chapter has presented ways in which you can begin to take charge of your unknown future and realize those dreams that have been percolating since you were a little girl. Like everything else in life, your wedding will probably turn out a little differently than you

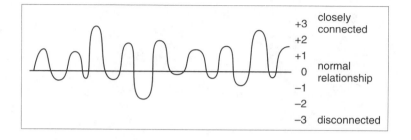

initially anticipated. The engagement phase will give birth to all sorts of surprising events and that can be a very good thing. The ability to survive prenuptial predicaments actually strengthens you against many future threats to your relationship. Why? Because when you actually start dealing with normal relationship struggles, you have begun the "work" of marriage.

COMMUNICATION—
IT'S A FAMILY AFFAIR

The wrens return
  each year to the
  house in the
  orchard
They have lived,
  they have seen
  the world, they
  know what's best.
For a wren and his
  wife
In the handsome
  house I gave
  them. They built
  their twiggy nest.
  EDNA
ST. VINCENT MILLAY

$\mathcal{M}$arriage represents one of the most complicated alterations in the life of a family, and integrating your future husband as a permanent member can be a weighty task. Unquestionably you want everyone to get along, and chances are that your parents and siblings truly want to love your partner as much as you do. Now is the time to begin the important process of bonding.

During this transition you may encounter some problems. The only way to defeat Murphy's Law—anything that can go wrong, will—is by rigorous planning and attention to detail. If issues emerge and you sweep them under the rug by pretending that things are pleasant, they will only crop up at a later time. Most importantly, do not take conflict personally! Remind

yourself that you all have a common goal. Ultimately, your family and your partner's family will cooperate in planning a beautiful wedding.

Families usually experience some friction when asked to integrate their child's romantic interest into their lives. Marriage is not just about two people who want to share their lives. Your family is required to expose themselves to a stranger, someone who enters the private world they have previously reserved for intimates. This outsider, your fiancé, is to be irrevocably joined, yet not by their own choosing.

Initially, everyone is on their best behavior. Your parents lay the table with their best china and everyone eats politely, without their usual squabbling. Your fiancé will also work hard at being liked, to fit in and be friendly. But after a while, people revert to their normal behavior.

I suggest that you advise everyone to adopt a slow approach in getting to know one another. If they have a common interest, like basketball, biking, or the ballet, make arrangements to spend time enjoying these activities together. It may be helpful to have your partner give his parents the same advice. Who knows, in time you might all even become friends.

PARENTAL BLESSINGS AND REJECTIONS

*K*evin: Mr. Rand, I'd like your permission to marry your daughter Connie.

Mr. Rand: You'll take good care of her, son?

Kevin: Certainly, sir.

Mr. Rand: Well, all right then. You have my blessing.

What was that, a passage out of Shakespeare? Believe it or not, throughout the ages and in most cultures, a man customarily asked his prospective father-in-law for his daughter's hand in marriage. In the not too distant past, your father may have hired a matchmaker to find you a proper mate and paid a handsome dowry to your future husband for taking you off his hands. With recent small advances in women's rights and the advent of greater autonomy for young people, it is now the norm for individuals to make their own choices. However, children of all ages still possess an instinctive need to please their parents, so it is not unusual to get a sense of a parent's approval before forging ahead with this major decision.

HOW TO HANDLE PARENTAL DISAPPROVAL

1. Remain calm and avoid reacting with anger.
2. Approach your family from a position of friendship.
3. Be willing to listen to their concerns.
4. Reiterate your allegiance to your partner.

Normally there are not any significant problems and you experience a smooth transition. But what if you don't gain parental approval? Worse yet, what if they disapprove? It is devastating to encounter such rejection. But should it stop you? First, try not to despair. Most likely their disapproval is born out of their fundamental reluctance to let you go and share you with another family. This is a very common response.

For most people, conducting such a dialogue with their parents yields cooperation and loving feelings. However, if your parents maintain their disapproval toward your future spouse, you will have to tell them straight out how you expect them to behave. You want them to be respectful of your choice, amiable to your fiancé, and make an effort to have a friendship of some sort. If they refuse, you will need to be clear about your primary loyalty to your partner.

It is not easy to choose sides, to be harsh with the people who have given so much to you, who kissed your forehead when you fell, who have supported you emotionally and financially all these years. Hopefully it won't come to that, but sometimes there is no way out. Let's face it, you are a real grown-up!

If you want your marriage to work, you are the one who will have to set the tone. Your relationship with your parents, though crucial, must come second to your relationship with your husband-to-be. A healthy marriage is one that has priority over all your other relationships. This is part of the process of shifting loyalties that getting married requires. That is what is meant by relinquishing your role as your parents' daughter. Getting your parents to accept your new role in their lives begins by you accepting this concept yourself. Then, recognize that as an adult you have the right and the responsibility to speak up for yourself with *everyone*. The key is to speak calmly, kindly, respectfully, clearly, and resolutely.

It is useful to remember that your parent or stepparent is doing the best he or she can to cope with the changes going on in your life. Hopefully, they will be able to hold up their end in maintaining or building a close relationship with you, their adult "child." If they are wise, they will know that there comes a time when keeping their reservations about your partner to themselves is the best course of action. If they do not, you may have to take action.

> You are much more important to your parents than you realize. When you take an assertive position with them, and back it up with action, they will take you seriously and will most likely be cooperative, if not immediately, then in time.

When David and Helene became engaged, there were some problems. David's parents were pleased as punch with their son's selection—a warm, educated, attractive New Englander. It was Helene's father who objected vociferously, expressing his belief that

his daughter could do much better than end up with a struggling law student three years her junior. He liked nothing about David, least of all what Helene loved best, his charming Southern accent.

"I don't care how much schooling he's had," her father screamed one day, "he's just not intellectual enough for you. It's a good thing your mother's not alive to see what her beloved child's ended up with, she'd die!"

Even as Helene and David focused on their wedding plans, her father's attitude never changed. Though he agreed to finance his daughter's nuptials, his criticisms did not cease.

Since she could not tell David about her father's attitude for fear of hurting his feelings, she came to see me.

"I just don't know what to think anymore," Helene began. "I love my father, yet he's behaving as if I'm committing the worst mistake of my life. . . . Do you think I am?" Crying throughout our first meeting, Helene also said, "I just know David is right for me. He believes in me, he encourages me to be independent, he treats me with love and respect. What more could I ever want in a husband?"

Helene made good sense and was in need of guidance to understand her father. As we talked about her family it became clear to us both that her father undoubtedly had his daughter's best interests at heart but simply could not treat her as an adult.

Helene realized that she always felt about five years old around her father. "No matter what man I would have chosen," she concluded one day, "Father would have found fault with him, because he just could not bear the thought that I've grown up enough to get married."

Helene and David's wedding was the most beautiful day of their lives. Although her father was a little grouchy throughout the event, he soon came to treasure his son-in-law as the wonderful person he truly was.

If your parents take a stand like Helene's father did, then you may need to assert your position as an adult who has the right to make her own decisions. Don't be surprised if their initial reaction raises doubts about your decision to marry. Your parents have had great influence over you, but that doesn't necessarily mean that they are always right. Parents use their own standards (and have their own psychological baggage) when judging your selection. You are not your parents and have your own criteria for choosing a spouse. Parents may sometimes be unable to comprehend their offspring's unique approach to life, her standards and needs.

What is called for is sympathy for your parents' difficulty in accepting your future spouse. Their future relationship with you and your partner will be greatly curtailed by their hapless attitude. Most parents don't want to be isolated from their children's life. What's more, access to their future grandchildren is at risk. The goal, of course, is to find a middle ground where you can freely exchange ideas with your parents regarding all of your important life decisions. Fortunately for most of us, we tend to choose our life partners wisely.

Ideally, parents would respect their grown child's wisdom when it comes to choosing romantic partners. With your relationship destined for marriage, it is doubly important that you and your parents work out an effective pattern of adult communication and behavior with a solid basis in trust and respect. Your assignment is to get on with the business of acting like an adult—be true to yourself!

How do you respond to unwarranted disapproval? Part of the maturation process for each of us is to become our own person and to be willing to assert who we are, what we want, and who we want to spend our life with. Otherwise, we are doomed to remain emotional children, under our parents' thumb.

In Chapter 1 the idea was introduced that conflict with your parents during this wedding planning phase is a crucial aspect of the transition from being their child to becoming your partner's wife. Letting go of people is the hardest thing we ever do, although over a lifetime we are required to repeat this many, many times. It is the human condition. Each stage of the Family Life Progression leads to the next. Conflict is a way of greasing the wheels of separation. It ensures that you proceed from your role as a child to the adult that you are.

There is a critical emotional shift between "dating" and getting married. This shift enables you to establish your new family with your husband-to-be. All the events that give rise to emotional upheaval throughout the wedding planning period—right up to and including your wedding day—are vehicles that carry you through this final transition from childhood to adulthood.

$\mathcal{N}$ancy came to her last psychotherapy session when she returned from her honeymoon. She was glowing with happiness as she recounted how wonderfully everything had turned out.

"Oh, I nearly forgot to tell you! You're not going to believe it, but remember how my mother was bugging me about the fact that I had decided not to carry a bouquet? It just seemed silly to me, you know. Anyway, we discussed it a million times. But, this is really the most outrageous thing you ever heard: She showed up at synagogue with a bouquet for me. Can you imagine? I refused it of course and I'm so proud of myself. Even though I was livid, I remembered to be assertive in a mature way. I calmly said, 'Mom, if you want to carry it, go ahead, but I'm not.' And then I walked away. Would you believe," Nancy exclaimed, "she didn't say anything further about it."

In this same vein of understanding how to deal with your own parents' disapproval, if your fiancé's parents

CONTINUING CONTACT

- Call, write, send greeting cards: Be persistent in your approach with your parents.
- Let them know that you are not rejecting them, only their values.
- Don't be surprised to get your letters back unopened.
- Expect your outreach to be rejected at first.
- If you are tenacious and allow your parents to save face, they will come around.

NINE STEPS TO SUCCESSFUL COMMUNICATION

1. Ask your parents to listen to you without interruption.
2. Begin by listing the specific reasons that are causing you to feel upset.
3. Back up each reason with details of incidents you have experienced.
4. Don't bring other people into this (such as,

(continues)

disapprove of his choice in you, understand that he suffers more than you. In such a case, it is wise to be supportive of your partner and avoid criticizing his parents. Censuring could lead to his need to defend them and turn him against you. The attachment between parents and their progeny is strong—do not underestimate it. Besides, if you let him have his own feelings then it will give him the emotional space to deal with things and hopefully resolve them.

When parents withdraw their love and approval—or perhaps even their physical presence—adult children can expect to go through a grieving process. It is natural to feel sad or depressed. Allowing yourself to experience whatever feelings occur assures their quick passage. But do not stop there: Become proactive. Follow the steps outlined in Continuing Contact and don't give up.

Relationships can be renegotiated, old unresolved issues can be addressed, and old standing patterns can be reshaped. When communication with your family has been restored, ask for your partner's support, figure out precisely what you want to achieve, and try Nine Steps to Successful Communication to obtain your goal.

Those you care about will eventually realize you have made a wise choice. Their acceptance makes your big step that much easier.

The pre-wedding period can be like the storm before the calm. Batten down the hatches now by bolstering your family relationships and hold tight to your partner. You will reap all the benefits.

YOUR NEW ALLIANCE

In choosing to marry you, your soon-to-be spouse has also inherited your family (and you, his). What if they don't get along that well? Or even worse, antagonize each other? What then?

$\mathcal{M}$ichael and Lisa came from entirely different backgrounds. Michael's family was intact, whereas Lisa's parents had each been married three times. Lisa's older brother had monthly emotional crises that promoted family upheaval and angst. To Lisa this was normal life. She had always experienced life as a roller coaster ride and was not thrown by her father's temper tantrums nor her mother's crying jags. Michael, on the other hand, was highly disturbed by her family's antics. Long after Lisa calmed down, as her mother's anxiety level returned to normal and her father apologized for his latest abuse, Michael continued to brood.

"I feel so uncomfortable with them," he told his bride-to-be. "The last thing I want is a close relationship with these crazy people."

"Well, Aunt Mary thinks . . .").
5. Be quiet and just listen as they respond to you.
6. Make some distinct suggestions that will allow you to reconnect with each other.
7. Ask them for feedback and suggestions.
8. Ask them to list their problems with the situation while you actively listen.
9. Make some tangible agreements about future behavior.

"What am I supposed to do?" cried Lisa during one of our couple sessions. "This is my family, I'm stuck with them, and unless you are willing to figure out how to integrate them into your life, Michael, I don't think we stand a chance."

Lisa was right. Michael had to find a way to accept her family and open up to them despite their dysfunctional routines. If you find yourself in a similar situation, try not to be thrown by the discomfort and anguish this may cause you. Like most people, your connection with your parents is undoubtedly important to you. What you would no doubt prefer is to blend your life partner with your family. But remember, once you marry nothing will ever be the same again—if you are doing things right.

This reality is what Lisa and Michael had to confront. For starters, Michael needed to recognize that there was no choice: Lisa's family was now his family, too. Once he accepted that idea, his resistance to his in-laws diminished. He began spending some quality time with Lisa and each member of her family. In this way they were more palatable to him. He also noticed some of their positive qualities. Lisa didn't rush Michael. Over time he grew to like her mother, tolerate her brother, and love her father.

Becoming a couple also requires that *you* alter your relationship with *your* family. Be open to changes that will probably be required in your new married life. For example, formerly you may have spent Sunday afternoons or evenings with your parents. Now that you are engaged, you may have to reduce your scheduled visits to one or two Sundays a month. Holiday times may also have to be curtailed in order to be fair to your fiancé and his family. Lisa's parents were initially upset at this change and claimed that they were losing their daughter. But Lisa persevered and in time they recognized the equity of the new arrangement.

Taking steps like these can be uncomfortable. However, think about all the married people who have survived the modifications made with their own families. As a matter of fact, it is a good idea to talk to others and learn what their experiences were like—especially your parents.

What if your partner is unreceptive to your family? Your course of action is somewhat different. As a newly established couple you need to put your heads together regarding an endless number of issues and decisions.

**ADOPTING A
GOOD ATTITUDE**

1. Listen to his point of view—without interrupting.
2. Try to understand the difficulty he is having in joining your family.
3. At the same time, be assertive as to your needs and reasonable expectations.
4. Make sure you give him plenty of time to acclimate to your family's style of interaction.
5. Remember, you are entitled to insist on your future husband's cooperation so that you can continue to have a loving connection with your family—albeit with some modifications.

What cannot be negotiated is whether your future spouse becomes a member of your family, or you of his.

Certainly, your fiancé cannot feel as close or as loving toward your family as you do. This would be too much to expect. If you want your partner to embrace your father or brother as his newfound best friend, then you are in for a great disappointment. (Although such wonders do occasionally occur.) What you can reasonably anticipate is that your partner will make every effort to be open to the possibility of friendship and, at the least, be sociable and respectful. In addition, he ought to be willing to make himself available to spend quality time with your family. But if your soon-to-be husband tells you about his difficulty being open to your family, try the steps in Adopting a Good Attitude.

Many couples fall into the terrible habit of being critical of each other's parents and siblings. In the beginning, chances are pretty good that you both have feelings of goodwill, perhaps even a fantasy about becoming one big happy family. The trouble often begins when you have had a confrontation with a member of your family of origin. Once you confide in your fiancé, he may become upset for you because he loves you.

Of course you want him to take your side, but if he is smart, he will not be critical of any member of your family. You certainly have the freedom to find fault with family members, yet, when someone else does, you experience a natural desire to defend them. Next thing you know, you are enraged with your partner instead of your parents or siblings. Certainly that was not his goal in supporting you. Yet, what your soon-to-be spouse has inadvertently managed to do is to allow you to deflect your negative feelings. This is a trap that can truly hurt a marriage—beware!

Where does that leave you? Can you confide in each other regarding family upsets? Of course you can. But instead of joining him in his anger toward his mother when she "bugs" him, learn to practice the highly effective Art of Active Listening.

IN-LAWS AND OUTLAWS

Most people clearly remember the first time they were introduced to their in-laws. According to the family therapist Jay Haley, what "distinguishes man from all other animals is the fact of having in-laws. All other animals mature, separate and mate on their own. Only man carries his whole family into the bargain. . . . Perhaps man has developed such a large brain in order to be able to cope with the complexity of his kinship system."

THE ART OF ACTIVE LISTENING

What: The ability to respond to what someone is saying to you by maintaining an emotional distance. This requires the listener to suspend judgment and subdue her resulting inner feelings or response. To use this tool successfully, it is particularly important to learn how to defer your own reactions.

Why: This way of communicating frees your partner to be honest with you and encourages him to reveal himself. Therefore, you can be completely available to be supportive of your partner's true feelings and concerns.

(continues)

Whether you met them before or after you got engaged, calm as you might have appeared, you were probably nervous and anxious to make a good impression. It is only natural to assume that you are being "sized up," that they are deciding if you are good enough for their darling child. You are bombarded by an endless stream of questions. You think twice about touching him too affectionately and you are very careful about what you say. Not that you are putting on an act—you are simply on your best behavior. Now would not be the time to mention that little birthmark on his bottom or the fact that his shower's water pressure is terrible. The best way to handle these early meetings is to just be yourself—the worst thing that could happen is that they may not initially like you.

Prospective brides should be cognizant of the pressure their future in-laws also experience during this phase. They have even more invested than you in having you like them. After all, they want to ensure the harmony of their relationship with their son. You are a very important player now that you are about to become his wife and perhaps the mother of their future grandchildren.

Chances are you met your future in-laws before your engagement. But something drastic changed when that ring was slipped onto your finger. You entered an entirely new family constellation whether you liked them or not. While you are accustomed to the quirks and quakes of your own family, you were suddenly faced with an assortment of strangers and their potentially upsetting and unfamiliar ways.

Sally-Ann's family was so proper that she often objected to the rigidity of her parents' style and how they strictly adhered to rules and regulations. But intimacy breeds a sense of ease, and Sally-Ann had learned to comfortably negotiate within her highly formal and somewhat cool family.

Strangely, we are attracted both to that which we don't have and to those who offer us a sense of familiarity. When Sally-Ann met Keith's family for the first time, she was excited about their outgoing, friendly, and relaxed ways—so different from those of her parents. Her future father- and mother-in-law warmed to Sally-Ann immediately. She loved their open and heated political debates over dinner.

When faced with wedding arrangements, however, the differences between the two families stood out in bold print. The formerly enjoyable arguments were now experienced as strikingly

How: Reflect, mirror, paraphrase, repeat, or summarize what you hear, as opposed to defend or fix.

Example:

He: I'm feeling anxious about dinner with my family.

She: So you are nervous about next week . . .

He: Yeah! You know what a pain in the butt my brother can be.

She: You really have a hard time with him.

He: I guess I'll just deal.

She: You'll figure it out as it comes at you.

He: Wow! You're so great to talk to. You really helped me. I feel better.

repugnant to Sally-Ann and to her family. Sally-Ann's subdued politeness got lost in the disorderly atmosphere of contrariness. It seemed to her that every detail was dissected, diced, and analyzed. Issues that she and her family handled with politeness, Keith's clan dealt with as a free-for-all.

For others like Sally-Ann, the foreign elements initially so alluring become strangely uncomfortable. People who were initially on their best behavior reverted to their real selves when key wedding planning issues were raised. Dealing with new in-laws can sometimes be confusing and uneasy.

Some people experience a different kind of problem. How do you manage to involve family without feeling overwhelmed by them? What if everyone gets along so well that it becomes relentless? Perhaps your future in-laws love you so much that you see them every weekend, when your own preference is to have more social time with friends or time alone with the man you love. Let's suppose your groom-to-be enjoys the super closeness. For one thing, you have a responsibility to your upcoming marriage to share these concerns with your partner. It is most important to be willing to tell him the

truth about your feelings—stand up to him, if necessary—and assert your fears and wishes.

If you are the one who has adopted your in-laws,
you might ask yourself if you are avoiding your own
family. Perhaps you are using your partner's parents as
a replacement in an effort to dodge difficult family
issues related to becoming a bride. Perhaps it feels as if
distancing yourself from your parents is the only way to
separate from them, or perhaps you are utilizing your
in-laws as a shield to avoid intimacy with your partner.
Try to be honest with yourself about this.

Surely the high level of stress during the transition
between singlehood and marriage can polarize a family.
It is easy to experience your parents as villains and
yourself as a victim. Avoiding the problem will not
work for long. Sooner or later the issues will reemerge
and will have to be dealt with.

You do not have to be best friends with your parents
or siblings—they may be too dysfunctional for you to
enjoy the fruits of a family friendship. Regardless of how
inadequate they may seem, however, it is in your best
interest to find a way to have some minimal connection
with them. Why? Because unresolved conflict with your
family will interfere with laying a solid foundation for
marital equilibrium. The quality of the connections with

Make it a rule never to say anything negative about his family and ask him to honor the same.

your parents and siblings determines your ability to successfully negotiate your intimate relationship with your partner—not to mention your future children

Then there is the drama of the first meeting between the two sets of parents. Get out the aspirin! In most cases, one of the mothers will initiate contact. They will congratulate each other and probably set up a date to meet—in your presence. If you or your parents or his parents are clinging to the fantasy that they will instantaneously become best pals, everyone is sure to be disappointed. The odds are heavily against it. But meet they must.

Many brides reason that since their parents and in-laws have so much in common, i.e., their children who love each other, there must be other areas of commonality. But think about it this way. Are you necessarily like your parents? Probably not. Would you choose them to be your friends if you were not related? Probably not! The best you can hope for is that everyone will become familiar with each other over time. After all, they have not chosen each other, you and your partner have.

If you are blessed, your parents and your in-laws will get along. Everyone will allow you the emotional elbow room to plan your wedding. However, most brides are not quite that fortunate. Even normally easy-going in-laws can become overbearing when it comes to wedding issues, for several reasons. Like your parents, they, too, want to be involved in all the goings on—that is a natural parental instinct. Although you are already an expert in dealing with your own parents' antics, dealing with your in-laws is virgin territory.

Your in-laws may feel they must have a say equal to that of your parents in order to keep things "fair." (It's starting to sound a bit like a tug-of-war, right?) You are likely to be slightly on edge yourself and more sensitive to their intrusion. And if things aren't bad enough, you know you have to tread gently because you are forming the groundwork of a new relationship.

The same holds true, more or less, for the relationships with your fiancé's siblings and friends. When you meet them you may be pleasantly surprised. You have a better chance of becoming friends with them since they are your contemporaries. Valuing your own relationships with your brothers or sisters enables you to make a greater effort in developing friendships with your future spouse's peer group. Your relationships with them could become great assets, lead to important friendships, and enhance the success of your marriage.

As an adult you realize that there are bound to be differences between you and your future in-laws. A healthy relationship is one that makes room for problems and finds functional ways to work them out. It pays to recognize that both sets of parents have their own feelings regarding your decision to marry, let alone your choice of a mate. Hopefully you will be able to view your partner's family as plain folks who have just as many assets and liabilities as your own family, only different. It takes time for someone to get to know you. If an individual takes an immediate dislike to you, it probably has nothing to do with you and everything to do with their own baggage. Give them time and exposure to you, and they will learn to like you for the wonderful person that you are.

If you suspect that your parents are upset about your choice of husband, it can't hurt to bring it out into the open. If it's your in-laws who seem to have an attitude problem, encourage your fiancé to approach them on his own. But don't expect to convince them of anything. It's enough sometimes just to air things out.

Bonnie: Mom, you just don't seem happy for me. Are you upset that we are spending less time together? Is it the cost of the wedding that's getting to you? Please just tell me!

Mother: Bonnie, darling, I am upset and just haven't been able to figure out how to talk to you about this without getting you all upset. After all, you are in love with Karl and you seem so excited about getting married, I'm reluctant to tell you what I feel for fear that you'll be furious with me.

Bonnie: Mom, you don't have to protect my feelings. You and I have a very strong relationship. Even if I get mad at you, we'll always love each other. I want you to tell me what's worrying you.

Mother: (taking her hand) I'm very concerned about the fact that Karl used to be . . . alcoholic. I'm worried he'll go back to drinking and ruin your life. There, I said it and I feel better.

Bonnie: (putting her arms around her mother) Thank you for your concern. But Karl is in recovery and I fully trust his commitment to his sobriety. I'm confident that as you get to know him better you will understand that.

> Great things are done more through courage than through wisdom.

An amazing process is set into motion when a formidable topic is addressed. By opening the door for conversation, Bonnie showed a lot of self-confidence, as well as strong feelings of love for both her mother and her future spouse. Just the process of sharing feelings, even when nothing else happens, is a relief for all concerned. When negative emotions are held secretly inside, they tend to block love and intimacy. Try opening up if you have not, and encourage your family to do likewise. Things will improve, I promise.

If your future in-laws prove difficult and your fiancé is swayed by their feelings, it may be time to take strict action.

After living together for two years and while driving cross-country in his Jeep, Jill and Tom made their decision to get married. The month-long vacation confirmed their belief in their compatibility. Returning from their trip, they announced their engagement to Tom's family. His father was delighted, shook his hand, and kissed Jill. His mother was less enthused.

As the wedding plans unfolded, Tom's mother became inordinately involved and pressed her future daughter-in-law to let her hair grow so that it could be put into a sophisticated knot. Jill laughed it all away, attributing the interference to a dominating personality that she wouldn't allow to affect her.

Tom, however, joined his mother in her campaign to change Jill, from the casual, comfort-driven woman that she was to an elegant ideal of a bride. Jill was often driven to tears by her fiancé's attempts at coercion. Soon, additional demands from her future mother-in-law were transmitted to her through Tom. Jill began to feel oppressed and resentful toward Tom and finally confronted him.

"I know you respect your mother's opinions, Tom," she said, "but if we are to have a healthy marriage it's time for you to let go of her. I am your partner, not your mother. It's my wedding, my hair, and not hers. I need you to be on my side, Tom, otherwise I will lose my desire to marry you."

Tom was struck by his bride's penetrating words, apologized for his insensitivity toward her, and asked her help in finding words to ward off his difficult, demanding mother. The bride was beautiful six months later, wearing flowers in her short, blonde curls.

It is each person's responsibility to handle his or her own parents and to set appropriate boundaries. If the love of your life is significantly influenced by his parents, then help him to perform the necessary work of becoming emotionally separate from his original family, in the service of creating a new family with you. With loving kindness and encouragement from you he will surely succeed.

MOTHERS-IN-LAW

One of the factors that creates such an aura of discomfort around the entire in-law issue is negative press given to mothers-in-law. Outsiders make great scapegoats. Your comfort level is always greater with people you know than with those who are new in your life. It is easy to view those who are on the edge of the loop as villains. It is harder to admit that your fiancé may have some difficulty with assertion than it is to be angry at his mother for pushing him around.

For your future mother-in-law, it may be easier to resent you than to admit her sense of loss at the time of your wedding. However, there is really no reason on earth to expect anything but a positive outcome with your fiancé's mother. She could become your closest ally as you embark on your role as wife to the man she gave birth to, and in turn, your favorite support with the children you may one day bring forth.

The relationship that women develop with their fiancé's mother can range from that of great affection on the one hand, to mere acquaintance on the other. What determines the two extremes is a complex cluster of personality traits. The daughter-in-law who is sensitive to her partner will make an effort to befriend her mother-in-law. Certainly, when you have a mother you are close to, your relationship with your fiancé's mother will be of a separate category. You will most likely experience her as a respected relative, unless you are fortunate enough to develop a closeness based on shared values and chemistry.

Your fiancé's mother's experience during your engagement period is totally different from yours. She is probably feeling as if she is losing her son to another woman. Her position as the most important woman in his life has been usurped by a stranger, someone who has woven a spell over her child. She may be feeling a very deep sense of loss at the same time that she feels joyous for both of you, because another part of her is grateful that her son has grown up. Hopefully, your future husband and his mother are working through their own separation issues, and you will note his ability to draw appropriate marital boundaries between her and his new family, namely you!

Your partner's mother's role in the wedding planning is most likely minimal; the same holds true for your fiancé's stepmother if he has one. Certainly your in-laws' wishes regarding the ceremony should be taken into account. After all, this event signifies a great change in their family structure as well.

If you and your future mother- or stepmother-in-law have developed a friendship, then perhaps you will want to include her in some of the legwork. Most often, her participation is limited to choosing her dress and throwing the wedding rehearsal dinner. She will be the delighted recipient of news bulletins from you regarding the details of the affair, but it is not mandatory to invite her input—it is your right as the bride to decide your colors, gown, flowers, and so on.

Under these circumstances, it is understandable that your future mother-in-law may feel left out. Her

FLOURISHING BESIDE
YOUR IN-LAWS

- On many levels, you
  will need to treat your
  partner's family as if it
  were your own. Both
  families will become
  involved with your relationship and will natu-
  rally want to include
  you and your spouse in
  family functions and
  holidays.
- Remember, his parents
  are just as important to
  your future husband as
  yours are to you.
- The better your relationship with your in-laws,
  the healthier your future
  marriage and family life.
- Your partner needs to
  have access to his family
  to ensure his emotional
  well-being. This will
  enhance, never detract,
  from your relationship
  with each other.

occasional overtures at friendship with you may be
motivated by her attempts to bridge the distance
between herself and her son. However, do not discount
her sincere desire to develop a good relationship with
you, the newest member of her family.

Your challenge is to be empathic to your soon-to-be
mother-in-law, maintaining your composure in the face
of what can feel like annoying interference. Think
about the advice given in Flourishing Beside Your In-
laws, and good luck!

IF YOUR PARENTS ARE DIVORCED

Parent and in-law issues are mild compared to the
histrionics that may occur if you come from a family (or
are marrying into one) where the parents are divorced.
Considering that approximately half of all marriages
have ended in a schism during the last twenty to thirty
years, there is a good chance that one or both sets of
parents are divorced. This section is designed to help
prepare you for this possible scenario: that your parents, or your beloved's parents, are divorced, hate each
other, and can't be in the same room together.

When Larry and Eleanor got engaged, all three sets of parents were thrilled. Eleanor's parents had undergone an ugly divorce

when she was three. A few years later, her mother, with whom she initially lived, suffered a nervous breakdown and was hospitalized. Eleanor moved in with her father, who had remarried. She and her stepmother loved each other—a good thing for a little girl who was estranged from her psychologically impaired mother throughout most of her childhood.

In time, Eleanor's mother recovered and remarried, and their relationship was repaired by the time Eleanor went off to college. A scar remained: Eleanor's parents hated each other, could never say a kind word about the other, and each resented Eleanor's love and loyalty to the other.

It was no surprise to Eleanor that the wedding planning process rekindled the rage. Eleanor was a practical person and in an effort to head off potential trouble began planning the details of her wedding a year in advance. As expected, the dirty laundry tumbled out early on in the process. There were many nights when Eleanor cried herself to sleep in Larry's arms over her father's cruelty toward her mother, her stepmother's demands for equal treatment, or her mother's onsets of depression. It was her worst nightmare come true.

But Eleanor's preventative measures finally paid off as the players came to terms with their various roles. She gave herself the time to address the difficulties that surfaced. Eleanor used her leverage as the bride-to-be to

Do not forget little kindnesses and do not remember small faults.

gain everyone's cooperation. In the end, she had a fairy-tale wedding where everyone behaved themselves.

It is the bride and groom's job to establish the rules and set the standards for decorum among diverse sectors of the family in order to survive family turmoil, have a beautiful wedding day, and ensure harmony. It is also your responsibility to be sensitive to the various factions in your highly complex family system. You may be surprised to find that if you behave with dignity and generosity (instead of lowering yourself to their level of immaturity and spite), even the most ill-tempered relatives will behave themselves. During a battle, a strong leader can motivate the troops to work together, leading them to victory. Somehow, a reminder of the uniqueness of the wedding day has a way of keeping people on their best behavior (or at least not their worst).

Remember, most friction erupts before the wedding ceremony, not during. Take your cue from Eleanor, anticipate family conflicts, take enough time before the wedding to head them off, delegate wherever possible, and demand that people rise to the occasion. And don't forget to save a little energy for the bouquet-tossing.

When Susan introduced wedding guests to her family she laughingly said, "This is my mother, and this is my mother, and this is my mother, and this is my mother," as she referred to her mother, stepmother, her new husband's mother, and his stepmother.

In the case of multiple divorces and remarriages, that's exactly what happens. How does the bride handle competition between two mothers-in-law for attention? My suggestion is that you ought to graciously accept the responsibility of developing separate relationships with each of your mothers-in-law. And beware: Never "triangulate"—do not discuss one with the other. (Triangulation refers to the dysfunctional pattern of getting in the middle of something that is none of your business or allowing others to pull you into what does not actually involve you directly. Gossip is the most dangerous form of triangulation.) Sometimes it is actually easier when both you and your fiancé come from divorced families. In this situation, each set can ally with a different set of in-laws.

Another confusion encountered by remarried families is the question of the etiquette and emotional repercussions of official meetings between divorced sets of in-laws. One bride-to-be wondered if it was appropriate to have her parents and in-laws together for their first encounter. Since her parents' divorce she had gained a comfort level in treating them as two distinct families. As such, she had excellent separate relationships with each of her parents and their spouses, never spoke to one set about the other, and even celebrated holidays and birthdays twice.

When she was eleven, Kristin's parents divorced. Except for her college graduation five years ago, there had never been a reason for everyone to come together. With the engagement and upcoming wedding, Kristin couldn't decide if the formula that had worked so well should be upheld.

After some consideration, Kristin reasoned that she was a member of good standing in two households—with her mother and stepfather *and* with her father. Each of her parents was separately involved with the wedding plans, including guest lists and finances. Therefore, it was most appropriate for her to continue this healthy approach. She suggested that each of her parents host a dinner where they could separately meet her fiancé's parents.

It can be confusing to be saddled with divorced parents. There is the potential for headaches and territorial bickering at every turn, and keeping the two sides clear of each other until your wedding day makes a lot of sense. If you find yourself ready to throw your hands up because of these intricacies—whether on your side or your fiancé's—remember that you would not be who you are today, nor fulfilled each other's dreams, had your families been more conventional.

HAMMERING OUT THE DETAILS

> I need to take an emotional breath, step back, and remind myself who's actually in charge of my life.
>
> JUDITH M. KNOWLTON

*T*he average engagement period in the United States is eighteen months. That's a very long time to be in a state of flux—it can strain friendships, family life, your career, your finances, and even your relationship with your partner. Ask anyone who has been engaged, they will tell you that planning a wedding can take over your life. Most people are just not prepared for how difficult and all-consuming it becomes. "This is supposed to be the best time of my life and look how stressful it is," said one client. There does not seem to be enough time for anything else and being a one-dimensional person can take its toll.

*A*nn became engaged in August to her boyfriend of five years. They scouted locations for their wedding every weekend, although it was fifteen months ahead. Evenings were spent on the phone interviewing caterers, rabbis, musicians, and photographers. They gave up time alone or with close friends in order to iron out the details of guest lists, finances, and the ceremony with their parents.

Not too long after these wedding plans were underway, Ann and her fiancé, Phil, began to notice that all this planning was stressing their relationship. Gone was the lighthearted fun and leisurely sex play. They began distancing themselves from single friends and gravitating to married and engaged ones. Instead of going to the movies, they brought home videotapes of bands for the wedding reception. Rather than exploring new vistas, they were checking out new china patterns. Agonizing arguments about arrangements were substituted for previously stimulating debates about politics. Romantic candlelight dinners gave way to meetings with their parents and prospective caterers.

On a whim, they checked to see if any earlier wedding dates were available at the location they had chosen. There was a cancellation and they snatched the earlier date. From there, planning went into hyper-drive. With no time to order a gown through the normal channels, the bride sketched a design out herself and brought it to a seamstress who finished the dress in only four short weeks. Handwritten invitations tied with white ribbon were out in two weeks. Flowers were ordered, the menu was set, and the small bridal party was outfitted quickly. There was no time for indecision, second thoughts, or family squabbles. And the wedding went off without a hitch—just like in the movies.

Ann and Phil could not cope with the trials and tribula-
tions of a lengthy engagement period. In many cases
this "all work and no play" phase can last longer than
the courting that precipitated it! If your wedding date is
set months or years into the future, try to avoid becoming one-dimensional wedding drones and keep your
relationship, your friendships, and your lifestyle upbeat
and fresh. If you focus on what is truly important, you
can maintain the fun and the romance during pre-wedding logistics.

WHO IS COMING TO THE WEDDING?

The only thing worse than office politics is family politics. Few things cause more headaches than the tug-of-
war that inevitably takes place between your partner,
yourself, and your families regarding whom to invite—
and whom not to. When your budget or the available
space is tight, finalizing a guest list can be a very frus-
trating experience. The following can assist you in managing the guest list:

What Do You Do If:

Your partner insists on inviting ex-girlfriends. If this
upsets you, and if your fiancé is still emotionally

attached to women from his past, then you will need to be open with him. Initiate a discussion, tell him your feelings, and actively listen to his reasons. In most cases, ex-girlfriends should remain in the past—but in life, everything can have exceptions.

Your parents are sulking because you told them they can only invite one table of friends. You may just need to let them have their feelings. Stick to your guns and don't expect that when you say "no" to someone about something they want, that they will be overjoyed.

Your in-laws (who don't even believe that the groom's family should contribute anything financially) want to invite 100 of their nearest and dearest. Once you and your fiancé make a decision about guest allocation, it becomes his responsibility to handle his parents. Let him do so, he could probably use the practice.

You are torn as to whether to ask people from your place of work. Depending on the number of guests you allow yourself, you will need to decide what purpose your wedding should serve. Does it need to be strictly personal? Is this also a political opportunity for you or for your future husband? Many people intertwine their friendships with work. If so, business associates could be invited.

Of all your acquaintances you only consider a handful to be real friends—can you omit the rest? Will there be future repercussions? Sometimes you just have to take a stand and like a real adult suffer the consequences of your decisions.

And what about the wedding party? You and your partner will have to agree on how many and which close friends and family members to include in this inner sanctum.

What if you have visions of an enormous entourage of bridesmaids, groomsmen, flower girls, and ring bearers, while your groom prefers only a best man and maid of honor? Chances are pretty good that what brought you together in the first place was a mutual caring and respect. Work it out and consider this to be a valuable opportunity to practice your negotiation skills.

What if you want it simple, but your mother wants your brother's kids to be in the wedding party? You don't have to get everything your own way. Even though it is your wedding, it is also a family affair and your parents' and parents-in-law's sensitivities ought to be considered. If you know that it will bring your mother joy to have her grandchildren actively involved in

Be prepared with tactful, firm responses that don't invite further conversation.

the wedding party, why not agree? In the end, you have to balance how badly you want one thing and how badly someone else wants another.

How do you tell Dad that you want to walk down the aisle alone? This is a tough one! A tradition founded on precepts that are no longer practical can still be meaningful. Once again, think about others as well as your own needs.

What if your annoying future sister-in-law thinks she should be matron of honor when you have already picked your best friend? Whom you choose to be in your wedding party ought to never be anything other than a personal matter. It is not easy to alienate a new in-law, but neither do you want to let anyone intimidate you.

Certain traditions of the marriage ritual are specific to some cultures, yet not to others. Some cultures limit their guests to the immediate family, whereas others, such as members of the Orthodox Jewish community, invite everyone they know, so that a typical wedding can easily consist of 400 people.

Howard and Joyce, a modern couple in the Orthodox Jewish tradition, decided to tie the knot despite his parents' disapproval. The groom's parents believed their son could do better, yet after some heated discussions with him they ostensibly relented. Howard foolishly told his bride-to-be about the conflict with his parents. Joyce felt deeply wounded, but elated that her fiancé's commitment was so hardy.

When both sides of the family conferred for the first time, Howard's father was consistently disruptive and disparaging of the many details that had to be ironed out. His parents took the traditional position that the bride's family was responsible for all of the expenses, yet they had a list of 200 guests that they wanted to invite. Joyce was in tears throughout the meeting. In the end, at Howard's insistence, his parents conceded to pay for the music and flowers. The wedding was beautiful. Although her parents could not really afford it, they went all out, and the 475 guests complimented the family on a successful affair.

Were there winners and losers at Joyce and Howard's wedding? You bet! Everyone lost. Joyce never forgave her in-laws for their lack of cooperation at the wedding. Four children later she was still harboring resentment, and Howard's parents missed out on a close and loving relationship with their grandchildren, daughter-in-law, and yes, their son, as he grew distant from them over the years. It is amazing how much wedding stress can influence a lifetime of relationships. Yet these and other

issues can be resolved through calm, rational communication and cooperation.

A CHAIR BY ANY OTHER NAME

Once you settle on whom to invite, you have to decide where to seat them. Be careful, seating arrangements are a lot like tea leaves—people tend to read a lot into them. Watch out if you relegate Great Aunt Jane to an inferior table in the back—you'll hear about it for the rest of your life. I know a couple who were seated at a table three feet from the too-noisy band and were so insulted that when the video photographer asked them to give their blessings to the bride and groom, they recorded a very nasty message instead.

Minutes prior to the ceremony, Kim's mother cornered her in the bridal room and begged her on bended knee to reconsider the seating. Kim and her sister, Sylvia, didn't get along. Sylvia had resented Kim since her birth—considering her, to this date, to be an interloper in her relationship with their mother. For many years Sylvia had embarrassed Kim, excluded her, and in general made Kim feel like an outcast because she was not married like Sylvia. Kim's revenge was to seat Sylvia near the kitchen with some boring neighbors.

She had stubbornly refused to stop the war and keep the peace for her mother. But when her mother's eyes filled with tears, Kim, who was feeling the happiest she had ever been, succumbed to her wishes. A smiling Kim walked up the aisle on her husband's arm, pleased that she had risen above such infantile behavior. Her sister was no longer such an important factor in her life. She was a married woman.

Old family issues often surface while you are hammering out the wedding details. The heightened emotionality of this time triggers unresolved problems to crop up, begging to be cleared. Be on the lookout for these land mines and you might be able to defuse the problems.

Consider this an unusual opportunity to mend fences, bond with those who have been distant, or start over again with others. Siblings like Kim and Sylvia now get a second chance to find peace with each other. Although Kim's relationship with her sister did not make a complete turnaround, their animosity decreased after the wedding. Don't look at the seating arrangements as a chance to get even; you could lose out on a great opportunity to smooth some ruffled feathers.

Establish some logical order to where you place folks, and in the words of Mr. Lincoln, remember that you can't "please all of the people all of the time." Both

What is it that you and your partner really want in a wedding? Zero in on what you would ideally desire. Sit down together with a pencil and paper and begin to answer the following questions and others.

- A small gathering or a huge event?
- A low-key affair or a real blow-out?
- Simple fare or haute cuisine?
- An afternoon gathering in the garden or a black-tie evening gala?
- A harpist, a disc jockey, or a ten-piece dance band?
- A wedding party or just the two of you?
- A synogogue or a catering hall?

sides of the family should be treated equally, older people should be near the dance floor but away from loudspeakers, and rowdy young people are happiest together—probably near the bar or the band.

A UNITED VISION

How extravagant should a wedding be? With all the hype, it is easy to lose sight of the true purpose of your celebration and watch it evolve into one that rivals the lavishness of Prince Charles and Princess Diana's. So before you agree to the ten-foot ice sculpture recommended by the banquet coordinator, stop, take a deep breath, and find your focus.

It is helpful to prioritize your preferences. Be sure to make your list a tentative one—you want to leave room for family input and change of heart. Call a meeting with all the parents and present your ideas together. Know in advance what areas you feel most adamant about. When your future father-in-law insists on having 300 guests, you can be open for compromise if you and your fiancé have put the size of the affair on the bottom of your priority list.

On the other hand, if your mother gives you a list of the cousins who simply must be included in the wedding party, and if number one on your list is that only a best man and maid of honor stand up with you, then you ought to take a stand about this issue. And you can be more flexible when your mother-in-law asks if she can wear black, which is her best color, even though you wanted everyone in pink, because that was number eight on your list.

Are your visions similar to your partner's? If not, how can you compromise on a wedding that will make each of you happy? When you both get stuck, how can you get out of the quagmire? What kind of control issues or power struggles can you unmask and resolve? You can negotiate successfully by utilizing a system of quid pro quo where both of you will be winners. This method consists of putting forth your own point of view, being willing to listen to your partner, and jointly discovering creative compromises where each of you gets some of your needs met.

Much of the "plain or fancy" issue is a reflection of the tastes and values of your family of origin. Realize that your future husband also has participated in family affairs and is probably imagining a wedding along those lines. This is one of the most challenging and troublesome aspects of getting married. You each may come from different backgrounds. The wedding is your first task to create a statement of yourselves as a couple and a family. Certainly, you will have different opin-

ions; you are two different people. Finding a middle ground and establishing a joint voice is the trick. Stay focused on that unified vision as you register for gifts, select the menu, and arrange all the details.

Like all major events in the Family Life Progression, weddings are filled with familiar rituals and traditions, not only for the participants in the ceremony but also for your guests. However, these days it has become accepted, and even expected, that most couples will deviate from tradition where gender equality issues are in question and other contemporary standards prevail. But as they say about modern art, it helps to know the rules before you break them. Certainly you should feel free to express your individuality, but a nod to tradition is comforting as well.

Breaking tradition can mean writing your own vows, wearing sneakers down the aisle, mingling observances from two faiths, wearing beige or pink instead of white, not throwing a bouquet, marrying under the stars, walking down the aisle with your mother, having a mixed-gender wedding shower, or any one of hundreds of other things.

As the bride, it is one thing to desire a break with tradition and another to assert your right to have your wedding your way. This is especially true when it comes to speaking up and saying what you want when you don't know your in-laws very well and you are still trying to make a good impression. Part of the difficulty is becoming accustomed to other people's styles of communication. Every family has an established and unique system regarding the discussion of differences, stating complaints, making requests, and giving opinions. It takes effort to decipher your new family's system, to conform to it when necessary, and to give up having things your own way when appropriate.

However, you may sometimes need to assert your point of view, possibly alienating your partner's family. This choice is risky since you have no guarantee that your husband-to-be will stand by you. This risk is quite worthwhile, however, if only to lay down the rules of the marriage early: The primary loyalty lies between husband and wife. If your future spouse takes sides with his family against you, take this as a clue that you two have a serious problem that needs to be resolved. Don't be afraid to insist on loyalty from your partner. Certainly you can disagree with one another. It's a question of *how* those disagreements are carried out.

Invitations are a ripe source of family conflict. They usually set the tone for a wedding and most people are traditionalists at heart in this area. Conservatively worded ones (i.e., "Mr. & Mrs. John Jones invite you to the wedding of their daughter Jennifer to Mr. James Johnson") usually foretell a traditional wedding celebration. But when a mere twenty percent of American households consist of the traditional nuclear family (according to the United States Census Bureau), then we have to be receptive to a wider range of nontraditional families as well as invitations. With so many different kinds of families, one often has to be creative with the invitations.

For example, in a family where the bride and groom may have four sets of parents between them, the traditional invitation may seem comical. "Mr. & Mrs. Robert Ryan, Mr. & Mrs. Frank Floyd, Ms. Madeline Chester, and Mr. & Mrs. Lawrence Miter invite you . . ." not only sounds silly, it doesn't leave enough room for all the vital information. Suppose some of the parents are remarried and some are widowed, divorced, or deceased. Perhaps your parents are cohabiting rather than legally married. What about homosexual parents?

The permutations are endless, and most young people who find themselves members of such families circumvent the problem by wording their invitations without mentioning *any* of their parents' names. This of course could cause contention from your parents or confusion for those invited, but modern circumstances demand unusual, creative solutions and often foreshadow an innovative wedding.

Most people share a desire to "express themselves" through their wedding celebration. One couple I know, both comedy writers, walked down the aisle together to the song "Send in the Clowns." Instead of hiring a limo, another couple I know made their grand exit on a motorcycle. Still another was married in a hot-air balloon high above their guests. Whether traditional or bold, the many choices you make for your wedding day cannot help but make a wonderful personal statement about the two of you.

"Patience is a virtue." It is also said, "Be careful what you wish for, you may just get it." Both maxims are quite applicable to wedding planning. After interminable months of waiting, organizing, and preparing for the big event, couples often come to the conclusion that the "perfect wedding day" is not all it's cracked up to be. The wedding-go-round is hard work, leaving you emotionally and financially drained and wondering if it could all possibly be worth it.

Pace yourself as best you can, moving from one "mini event" to the next until finally you reach "the big day." These mini events are like dress rehearsals for the

> Your marriage and your wedding do not have to be like anyone else's.

real thing. They include buying the ring and showing it to the folks, registering for wedding gifts, having an engagement party, taking an engagement photo, obtaining the marriage license, being fitted for the gown, ordering the tux, and dealing with your future husband getting drunk, or worse, at his bachelor party. Even something so seemingly civilized as the bridal shower is fraught with its own set of complexities.

Traditionally, the female community participates in the shower ritual as a symbol of support and acceptance for the soon-to-be bride. In contemporary circles, women also have bachelorette parties where they go out drinking with a few good friends on the night of the groom's bachelor party. Although these are great opportunities to enjoy the sisterhood of women and stock up on kitchen gadgets or sexy lingerie, many of the key players may harbor unexpressed concerns.

You, *the bride,* who hates to be the center of attention, may frequently feel embarrassed by your mother's lack of tact or sophistication, by your future-sister-in-law's attempts at humor, or by some of the gifts you get.

Your *mother,* who never had a proper shower and wants yours to be picture perfect, may feel uncomfortable with your overt sexuality as she watches you unwrap gifts of sexy lingerie. Although you may see a side of her you never suspected. At one family shower, the mother of the bride, slightly buzzed from champagne, began modeling her daughter's gifts. Everyone was in stitches as she sashayed around in sheer black held up over her pantsuit.

Your *groom's mother* or your *stepmother,* who wants desperately to be part of things and perhaps feels left out of your inner circle of family and friends, delights you when she suggests that everyone present take turns giving you, the bride, sage marital advice. And then her best friend clues you into a terrific guerrilla tactic—when you are losing an argument with your partner, just take off all your clothes.

Your *sister,* who is also the maid of honor, may secretly wish that she was the one getting married instead.

Your future *sister-in-law,* who feels hurt that she has no role in the wedding, but has hosted the shower anyway, has really stepped up a few notches in your opinion. Who knows, you may give her the honor of witnessing the signing of your vows.

As you can see, the psychological underpinnings of each and every mini event in the wedding cycle can be quite complex. That is why so many couples describe the culmination of their wedding day as a mixture of joy and relief. Indeed, I have heard people compare wedding planning to childbirth. It is not much fun while you're doing it, especially near the end, but then suddenly it has great meaning—that one glorious moment when you turn and walk back down the aisle as husband and wife, all the trouble seems worthwhile.

A SPECTRUM OF CULTURES

In the early phases of dating, people often dismiss the importance of religious or racial differences. But when they make the permanent commitment of engagement, problems that have never been addressed may surface. The differences that did not seem to pose challenges suddenly can. Parents who had acted agreeably sometimes sing a new tune of disharmony when the relationship becomes official. Couples from different religious backgrounds face the task of combining diverse wedding rituals, and couples who were previously color blind must deal with the realities of joining people of two races. People begin to think about raising children, sharing holidays, and combining value systems.

Marriage, a most difficult *and* rewarding institution, unites two highly dissimilar beings: a man and a woman. Other differences that exist beyond gender can add further complexities and stress to the relationship. Generally, the more similarities that exist between two people, the more likely their compatibility. Of course you and your fiancé each come from a different family, with its own traditions, history, rules, myths, experiences, and dysfunction. It is truly amazing that marriages work at all.

The good news is that you can successfully share your life with someone who did not grow up in a family just like yours. However, the more your past and his match, the easier will be your marital adjustment. Obviously, a man who is of a different religion, race, or culture from yours possesses stacks of incomparable experiences. Since getting married also involves the joining of two families, it is understandable that intermarriage is a highly charged event for all concerned.

This section of the book will assist you in overcoming some of these very difficult religious, cultural, and racial obstacles. How do you deal with your parents when they tell you that the love of your life *offends* them because of his cultural background? How do you deal with in-laws who try to stir up trouble between you and

> From the moment of birth, the customs into which an individual is born shape his or her experience and behavior.

your intended? How do you keep your love alive as your parents attempt to break you up? Is it necessary to stay in contact with family when all you get is heartache? Are you marrying your beloved, or his entire family?

Let's begin by shedding some light on what motivates your parents, and what their thinking might be in all of this. Don't forget, in order to create good working solutions it helps to gain an understanding of the underlying issues.

Your parents, who dearly love and cherish you, may be feeling betrayed, guilty, and threatened. Their religion or culture may be a fixed part of their lives, and they may have a high degree of commitment to its principles. You, their child, are an integral part of their heritage. Your parents may feel you have negated their powerful beliefs in choosing a totally different path. They may not know how to come to terms with an offspring who, from their perspective, disregards or mocks their belief system. They also may feel guilty, that they have failed in some way. Even though your parents want to trust you and your decision regarding this life choice, they feel helpless.

Some parents, limited in their outlook, cannot easily integrate a whole set of new relatives of another color or religion. Remember Archie Bunker? Parents may have difficulty overcoming their pain about their child's perceived tainted future. Parents need to face whether they can still be true to themselves while loving and accepting you, their adult child, *and* your intended. In addition, they need to find a way to accept the path you have chosen rather than what they always wanted for you. Some parents have so much obstinacy regarding intermarriage they have gone so far as to disown their child.

Mrs. Boyle, an Irish-American woman, called me one day to ask for a session because her husband was threatening to disown their thirty-six-year-old daughter, Maureen, after she had announced her engagement to Charles Wong, a forty-year-old Chinese American.

I eventually met with Mr. and Mrs. Boyle, Maureen, and Charles, during a family therapy session where the Boyles were shocked to learn that Charles's parents were also angry at his choice for a mate. He reported that his parents were pressuring him to reconsider and call off his engagement. They refused to even meet Maureen as they contended that only a Chinese woman would respect family traditions.

Mr. and Mrs. Boyle took an immediate liking to their future son-in-law and became absorbed in brainstorming toward a solution to helping him deal with his family. In time, Mr. and Mrs. Wong also came to appreciate their son's choice in a mate, although there were occasional grumbles of disapproval about their daughter-in-law's Western ways.

Something about a wedding brings out the Irish in people. Or the Jewish. Or the Baptist. More than any other event, a wedding brings to the surface the desire to protect one's religious and ethnic traditions. When it comes to the ritual and its symbols—the details of the ceremony, the bridal party, and the reception—normally level-headed people can become territorial, emotional, and unreasonable.

Deciding whose family minister will perform the ceremony is difficult enough when the bride and groom are of the same religion. But imagine resolving a decision between a Jewish rabbi and a Catholic priest, a Baptist reverend and a Lutheran pastor, a Greek Orthodox priest and a layman cleric. More and more families today face such issues as their children enter into interracial, interfaith, and intercultural marriages. Indeed, it is a fact of life that most progressive churches and synagogues are adapting to.

One couple recently faced just such a dilemma. His family was Jewish and hers was Roman Catholic. Neither of them was particularly religious, but when it came time to organize the ceremony, they each wanted to respect the sensitivities of their families. Unable to be married by either a conservative rabbi or Catholic priest (neither would recognize the marriage), they were wed by a Jewish Reconstructionist rabbi. As a concession to his family, the ceremony took place on a Sunday in October rather than on Saturday, the Sabbath day. As a concession to her family, the female rabbi suggested that the short ceremony be delivered entirely in English and that skull caps need not be worn. In this way, each family was asked to compromise a little, but both felt that they had sufficiently protected "their turf." They were rewarded with a beautiful balmy day, a romantic outdoor ceremony, lots of loving family feelings, and a joyful bride and groom. Unfortunately, some intermarriages do not work as well.

Salam, a Muslim from Egypt, and Norma, a Christian from Lebanon, didn't intend to fall in love when they were both involved in a New York business venture.

Each came from a highly traditional family where it was prohibited to marry outside one's faith and culture. Norma had always thought that she would one day marry a man from her community, and it was the same for Salam, who had expected that his parents would eventually find him an appropriate bride from among their group.

After several years and a great deal of consideration and pressure, Norma converted to Islam and changed her name to Fatamah so that the two could marry. The couple met extraordinary opposition from both their immediate and extended families. Only Salam's mother attended the dispirited wedding, which took place

HELPING YOUR PARENTS ACCEPT INTERMARRIAGE

1. Let your parents know that you have given cultural and racial differences more than adequate consideration. Perhaps share with them your own educational process in learning how to make intermarriage work. Give them specific examples of what you and your fiancé have worked through in terms of wedding details, future children, and holidays.

   (continues)

in New York City. Norma's family and Salam's father said they could not make the long journey to America.

Differing traditions can be one of the sorest subjects of any wedding and can truly cause remarkable damage to the fabric of a new marriage. Norma and Salam's story was a sad one. For three years after they wed they suffered greatly—experiencing inexplicable distance and irreconcilable differences. On the verge of divorce, they came to see me. Once we pieced together the details of their wedding fiasco, they were able to mend the tear between them.

WHO IS PAYING FOR THE WEDDING?

Why is money the single greatest arena for conflict and the basis for so much wedding stress? Clearly, the cost of making a wedding can be astronomical, often producing overwhelming emotional reactions.

In the past, tradition called for the parents of the bride to foot the bill. This tradition was rooted in the widespread belief that a daughter was her father's property. As such, she was an asset and a liability. She was an asset in that she could be used as a bridge to connect one family's wealth and influence to another and through progeny continue the family's status. Her liability was that her worth was measured by her value as a marriageable object that fattened her father's coffers. An old maid was viewed as an extra mouth to feed.

The dowry was utilized as a way to sweeten the pot for the prospective groom, who then effectively "owned" her. Hence the tradition of the bride's father literally "giving her away" to host the celebration for this event. As you are well aware, women have rebelled against being treated as men's chattels, also affecting society's attitude toward the marital tradition. Today, in Western society, women and men choose their mate, and most people marry for love rather than money.

Positioned with these changes, the groom's family began to take a more active role in the wedding ritual. These days it is common for the groom's family to at least pay for the music, flowers, and/or photographer, while many share the wedding expenses equally with the bride's family, and still others foot the entire bill when economics are an issue. On the other hand, many couples choose to pay for their own wedding. This is especially true when the bride and groom are

2. Be sensitive to your parents' struggle in coming to terms with this issue. Give them time to deal with their fears of loss regarding their relationships with you and their future grandchildren.
3. Again, be sensitive, respectful, and patient. Potentially explosive issues can either be resolved to the satisfaction and delight of all involved, or at least managed with a reduced amount of stress.
4. Above all, keep the lines of communication open.

older and more established or when marrying for a second time.

What is it about money that makes it such a delicate subject? Money is one of the most powerful elements in our social structure. Yet, despite the fact that you can't live without it, most people shun talking about it. In everyday life money is an object we exchange for merchandise and a variety of services. However, money also has some weighty emotional ramifications that are both positive and negative. Depending on our cultural background, we associate money with security, freedom, control, power, love, self-esteem, embarrassment, dependency, and happiness.

Each family has its own unique history and meaning related to money. Growing up in your family has instilled in you an entire set of attitudes and beliefs about the significance of money. In some families money is for saving, in others it is for fighting, or winning, or hoping, or worrying, or for keeping secret. Whatever your conditioning has been, this transmission has induced you to either imitate your parents' attitude (if you are a compliant person) or to go completely the opposite way (if you are rebellious).

In many families money and power are synonymous. When it comes to weddings some parents exercise control through their generosity, getting involved with every detail. Indeed, for the price of a big, fancy wedding some parents expect to "run the show." From the guest list to the hors d'oeuvres, to who walks down the aisle with whom, these misguided folks think that they can buy love, respect, and gratitude from their grown-up children.

What drives such parents is a basic insecurity that is most likely a function of unresolved issues from their own families of origin. Basically, people with an intense drive to control have experienced deep psychological trauma as children. They had no control whatsoever over others or their environment, or were involved in debilitating circumstances such as the death of a parent or of a sibling, physical or sexual abuse, abandonment, war, and so on. They were once helpless and truly suffered for lack of control and power.

Adults with such formidable childhood experiences make every effort to prevent the repetition of their ghastly feelings of helplessness. They want to be in control of all the changes in their lives. Parents like these tend to infantilize their children, yet believe they are motivated by love. They unconsciously reason that they need to protect their offspring to ensure that they will be insulated from harm, hurt, or deprivation.

> Assertiveness is the art of polite repetition that does not allow for the deflection of your goal.

What are the best ways to deal with parents and in-laws who try to control your wedding with their checkbooks? First, try to grasp their motivation—could it be insecurity? You don't have to take it personally since it is not about you. Your parents may be treating you like a child because of their love and distorted concern for you, not because you are incompetent.

Second, don't get wrapped up in your parents' financial manipulations—rise above them. How? Realize that your parents are doing the best they can, burdened as they are by their emotional baggage. Sit down with them and actively listen to their personal concerns regarding your wedding. And then spell out the ground rules— what you are willing or unwilling to compromise— *before* accepting their money. You probably won't be met with immediate compliance, but if you repeat yourself often enough it will eventually work. You are an adult, act like one!

Some brides and grooms confront parents who are totally unwilling to compromise their wishes. In such a case you have but two choices: Either capitulate to their point of view and allow them to have the wedding of *their* dreams (a big mistake) or refuse to accept their funds and make your own wedding. This may seem harsh to you, but sometimes you have no choice but to take matters into your own hands. In the end, you may not have the wedding you always wished for but at least it will be truly yours. And your self-respect will be left intact.

How much should you expect your parents to be willing to spend on your wedding? Supposing you want an incredibly sophisticated affair and your parents either can't afford it or are philosophically opposed to such an expenditure? What do they owe you? Here's the scoop: Your parents don't owe you anything anymore. You are an adult and it's all up to you. However, because they have an emotional investment in greasing the wheels of the family life cycle, most parents do feel an obligation to provide funds for their child's nuptials.

But have they, as the underwriters of this gala, come to terms with sharing the decision-making with you, your intended, and your in-laws? Will they gift you the funds? That could certainly ease the process. What happens when your future in-laws are willing or able to spend more on this wedding than your parents can? This is what happened when Lynn and Sam planned their wedding.

The families embarked on their initial discussion one fine Friday night over dinner. Both sets of parents were delighted with

their child's choice of mate and excitedly participated as everyone tossed out ideas about the big event. The bride's parents had saved about $10,000 over the years and initially felt pleased with themselves with this generous sum.

Pleased with themselves, that is, until the groom's parents, who were considerably more wealthy and had already thrown a wedding for their older son, educated them as to the reality of the high cost of an elegant celebration. Then the groom's parents offered to underwrite it in its entirety. The bride's parents refused on the grounds that it was their responsibility to pay for the bulk of the wedding. In the end, the two sets of parents negotiated the following arrangement.

The groom's parents offered to lend $35,000 to the bride's parents and also pay separately for the music, flowers, photographer, and honeymoon. In this way, the bride's family could pay for the remainder, including the costs of the church, pastor, reception room, caterer, libations, and bridal gown. The children could have a beautiful affair and there was supposed to be no hurry to repay the loan.

Six months after the wedding, the trouble started. Sam's father had a private talk with him one Sunday afternoon. "Has Lynn's father mentioned anything about settling the loan?" he asked his son. Almost immediately everyone became involved in the family feud. The young couple was torn apart as their parents battled over the debt.

Lynn and Sam came to see me. Their marriage was disintegrating because each was taking sides with their respective parents.

As you can see, fiscal politics are highly charged with feelings of anxiety, competition, and loyalty and can be a continuing danger to the well-being of your future marriage. For Lynn and Sam money also was a trigger for "triangulation."

> The course of true love never did run smooth.

Triangles are dysfunctional ways of interacting with other people. You learn these unhealthy communication patterns in your family. They occur when an issue that involves just two people brings (triangles) a third (person or thing) into their relationship (or communication). This helps lessen the conflict in the initial twosome. For example, if you and your fiancé have an upsetting incident and instead of talking it out with him you tell your mother, you are triangling her into your relationship with your partner. This injures your relationship with your partner, who becomes the villain, as it allies you and your mother against him.

Lynn and Sam's unfortunate situation resulted from the formation of a destructive triangle. The loan agreement was between the two sets of parents. When they dragged their children into the situation, they triangulated them and inadvertently created two camps—in this way the young couple's loyalty returned to their families of origin, instead of being upheld between them. The tension decreased for the parents with the involvement of their children, but increased for the newly married couple. Family therapists who have studied the dynamics of healthy and dysfunctional interactions between intimates have ascertained that when people communicate with each other directly, one on one, their relationships are close and well-functioning.

When discussing wedding finances, you should be aware of the ultimate effect on other participants. For the health of your future marriage, be on the lookout for triangles and refuse to participate in them! For example, it would be a mistake to rave about how generous your parents have been in front of your future in-laws, or vice versa. That's actually a triangle and may cause unnecessary resentment.

Like the national debt, the average cost of a wedding in this country is spinning out of control. Most weddings—excluding the engagement ring and the honeymoon—range from around $10,000 to $60,000. (There are also people with great wealth who spend much more and those who prefer to spend much less.) That could be the price of a new car, two years of college tuition, or a big dent in your family's savings. No wonder the topic gives so many engaged couples angst.

Assuming you have some money, can get it, or can put it on credit (many couples do), it is still no easy chore to decide where it is best spent. Let's face it, most of our budgets are limited. That means prioritizing your wish list and adjusting your expectations to fit fiscal reality. You may have to choose a less expensive gown, a smaller guest list, a cash bar, or a wedding at home. Each of these issues can cause disagreements or create grudges between you and your partner, parents, or in-laws.

And so you find yourself facing the psychology of economics, as well as your individual relationship with money. Most people are more comfortable discussing their sex life than their bank account. Ask a man how much money he earns and in most cultures he'll decide you are a rude boor. What is it about how much money we have, or how we choose to spend or save it, that raises our anxiety level?

How do you deal with the people in your life who stand between your dream wedding and fiscal reality? You are an adult, and as such you will sooner or later be confronting the limitations that life offers. It's nice to have a fantasy, but then it's time to join the real world and take your parameters into consideration.

How do you manage your own feelings about what you want and what you can have? Certainly you may

For every evil under the
sun,
There is a remedy, or
there is none.
If there be one, seek till
you find it;
If there be none, never
mind it.

feel disappointed when you cannot have things entirely your own way. And by all means, you are entitled to have your feelings. After all, no one shouts hooray when they cannot have what they want. But then it's time to talk to yourself like a good friend and make compromises.

If you adopt a creative, constructive attitude to the planning, you may be able to stop singing the wedding budget blues. Consider booking your wedding "off season," asking a friend to be your photographer, having the reception at the beach, or serving a homemade cake. In other words, let your personalities, not your budget, make your wedding day special.

THE QUESTION OF ELOPEMENT

Sometimes a formal wedding is not feasible. But is elopement—where the couple surreptitiously, or with one or two witnesses, gets married—ever a good choice? Most frequently, people elope for two reasons: Either their families disapprove of their marriage or there is an inordinate amount of conflict surrounding the wedding plans. Eloping is viewed as a way to circumvent antagonism.

Diane's mom wanted to make her daughter the most beautiful and sumptuous wedding money could buy—in other words, to have the kind of affair her own mother couldn't afford to give her when she had married Diane's father. Diane's parents separated when she was a baby and though he had children with another woman her father had always supported Diane and even now wanted to help out with the wedding. Diane's mother had ideas about the kind of dress her daughter would wear, the ice sculpture on the buffet table, the matching hot pink dresses for the four bridesmaids. She had even chosen the cutaway for the groom. Diane and her fiancé had their own ideas about what they wanted, but Diane's mother wouldn't hear of them.

After another raging debate regarding what *her* mother wanted and how *their* wishes were being ignored, Diane and her intended met at city hall on their lunch hour for a clandestine ceremony.

Did Diane make the right decision in getting married without family or friends present? Research indicates that marital adjustment will be more difficult for people who have eloped. Weddings are intended as rituals that assist the transition in the family and foster resolution for an abundance of pre-existing issues. The process of joining two families has significance for every member involved, not just for the bride and groom.

Was history repeating itself already? Diane did not consider her mother's feelings when she decided to elope, just as her grandmother had disregarded her mother's wishes when she married Diane's father. Might Diane's mother's anger at her own mother, and disappointment in her own wedding, have had a bearing on Diane's parents' divorce? Were Diane's parents deprived of a healing opportunity to launch their daughter into the adult world? Was Diane deprived of her last chance to be fully in role as her parents' daughter?

To all these questions I think the answer is yes. But let's not forget one of the most crucial factors lost to both Diane and her husband: The chance for mother and daughter to work out their adult-to-adult relationship, and for Diane to demonstrate her separate status as part of a couple by standing up to her mother regarding those wedding details that were important to her and her partner. These issues will not disappear just because the wedding was circumvented. When the sheen wears off the marriage vows these issues will reemerge with a greater force than ever.

Elopement is a good choice only when you do not have a family or too many friends. Even if you would prefer to spend your assets on something solid, such as a house or a car, rather than a five-hour party, there are ways to tone down a wedding. Some people enjoy a very small wedding consisting of only the immediate family, with a reception-like party to follow. Others skip right over to a honeymoon at the Waldorf. Still others accept whatever funds their families are willing to contribute as a wedding gift, use it toward a large purchase, and take everyone out for dinner after the ceremony.

No matter what you plan, it is important to keep in mind that your wedding needs to be witnessed by family and friends in order to gain emotional legitimacy. Certainly you ought to please yourself and your partner. But also remember that getting married is a rite of passage that has a long history of meaning. The pomp and circumstance is an extremely important event in the life of your family. If you can help it, do not cheat yourself, or them, of this special event.

Sometimes people get scared away from the pleasure of a formal wedding because of the dreadful experiences that others may have had. If you have considered elopement in order to avoid the hassles that a wedding often entails, I don't blame you for dreaming of escape. But you don't have to take the coward's way out. If what you really want is a beautiful wedding day, then do not deprive yourself of the lasting memory of an attended wedding with all the trimmings.

*L*inda's brother's wedding had turned into a complete fiasco when her mother refused, the night before, to walk down the aisle with her ex-husband, Linda's father. The turmoil that ensued when her brother challenged this demand nearly ruined their beautiful wedding. Although Linda was accustomed to intermittent divorce aftershock, she was devastated by her mother's antics.

When Linda and Josh decided to marry, her inclination was to elope for fear of a repeat performance. Josh, however, didn't want to deprive himself and Linda of the value that only a real wedding can provide. He and Linda put their heads together, and Linda decided to confront her mother.

"I'd like to have a big wedding, and I know that's something that would make you happy, too. But Mom," she said, "I'm really fearful of having something terrible go wrong as it did at my brother's wedding. Frankly, I'm thinking of eloping. What do you suggest?"

"I also feel terrible about what happened," her mother replied. "But please, don't let that stop you from having the kind of wedding you really would like."

"All right, Mom, I'll go ahead and plan a big party and I'll take your feelings into consideration. But I need your promise that you will not start anything," she asserted.

"You've got my word!" said her mother.

Linda's mother kept her word. She behaved socially toward Linda's father at the wedding. However, her sister-in-law instigated a major family feud by complaining about having to leave her three-month-old baby with a sitter—even the best of wedding days are never perfect. The hours before the wedding were a bit stressful for Josh and Linda, but they made it through and were glad they had decided not to elope

To minimize your conflicts, you could begin by letting go of the myths that surround this time. There will be issues! Think of this time as an essential moment to work out family relationships. The more successful you are at resolving the underlying problems between you, your parents, and your siblings, the greater is your potential for marital happiness and for a well-adjusted new family constellation. Isn't this what you ultimately want? By following the suggestions outlined in this book you will maximize your success. You may still have to contend with a handful of knots, but as long as you work through the potential pitfalls, they will not have the capacity to spoil your day.

MOTHERS AND DAUGHTERS

She wants to live for once. But doesn't know quite what that means. Wonders if she has ever done it. If she ever will.

ALICE WALKER

*S*andra and her fiancé had decided on a simple affair. They opted for a buffet since they hated the waste that most weddings presented when a lavish cocktail hour was followed by four courses that were never eaten. They also believed that people got glued to their seats and limited their socializing during a sit-down dinner.

Sandra's mother got riled when she couldn't convince her daughter to alter this format. "What are people going to say?" she cried. "None of my nieces or nephews ever had a problem with a normal wedding. What's wrong with you?"

"Mom, take it easy," soothed her daughter. "It'll be good, you'll see. We won't have tons of leftovers to worry about and it will be a lot cheaper."

"Ha! That's what you're saying, I'm cheap. Maybe we shouldn't have a wedding at all."

"I never said you were cheap, Mom," a concerned Sandra responded, "that's just how Chris and I want things."

"Next thing I know," screamed her mother, "you won't want to wear white! Young people these days don't understand the importance of tradition. Everyone I know got married in a church, and then we had a sit-down dinner. Your ideas are crazy—you'll embarrass me. Everyone will think we're cheap and that's why we're not feeding them properly."

Sandra was flustered, yet not surprised. She knew that her mother was a traditionalist and was influenced by her own experiences. Sandra also knew that her mother loved her. Sandra's high degree of self-esteem allowed her not to take her mother's reactions too seriously. And she was able to distinguish that it was, in the end, her wedding. Although she wanted to please her mother she felt it was appropriate to stand her ground, insisting on the details that were especially important to her and to her fiancé.

Mothers and daughters are, as the journalist Liz Smith says, "natural allies (as well as) natural enemies." No one up until now has been as important to you as your mother, nor been loved as much by you, even if you may not like or respect her. The tie between you is inexorably charged with expectations and possibilities.

What makes this connection so powerful? Because of your shared genetics and gender—you probably look and sound alike—and because she also has been your female role model, you may even act and think alike.

As with all role models, we admire them, simultaneously competing to be better or different, and we eventually need to separate from them emotionally. Why? Because a universal survival mechanism determines our need to detach, but at the same time we have a concomitant need to stay connected. Our relationship with Mother may be loving and friendly or hostile and anxious, but at our center is a need for her to always love us unconditionally and to be available to us should we falter.

THE DANCE OF SEPARATION

Your wedding is a time for you and your mother to renegotiate your relationship. You will hopefully move from being dependent on her to being self-determined and interdependent with your future husband. Not needing her as much can free you from judging her or seeking her constant approval.

No matter how difficult your mother may be, the process of getting married provides countless opportunities to resolve mixed feelings about her and about yourself. It's time to grow up, to let go of your fear, blame, and anger toward your mother and to replace it with recognition of who she really is, and who you really are: A woman who loves her mother, appreciates the relationship with her, and simultaneously regards herself as an independent adult.

The dance of separation from your mother can be choreographed most effectively during the engagement phase. It began with taking a few steps away from her while you were dating in your search for a mate. Now that you are engaged, you and your mother move closer together as you shape the ritual that will join you with your partner. This seems a practice as old as time, an experience that is familiar to your mother.

She is accustomed to taking your hand and leading. You step to the left, hoping she will follow as you state your preferences for this and that. She takes a few steps back, expecting you to drift in the same direction. You take her by surprise and lead her toward your favorite colors, flowers, and rites. You struggle. Sometimes the rhythm of the dance encourages cooperation as you let go and move to your own melody. In such moments you are freed up to follow your own tempo, while she can experiment with new movements. And, periodically, you come together in loving friendship.

Executing the dance of separation between you and your mother includes applying balance and tolerance to meeting your needs. Your mother would love to be intensely involved in your wedding plans if you let her. To her it will feel like a junket—exciting and fun to share this task with you. Her feelings of loss will be minimal if you and she have a fairly good relationship. This will offset the strong emotions she may have regarding the void that you are leaving between her and your father. If she is divorced or widowed, this family process may be even more difficult. The more she is able to recognize the presence of underlying issues that are raised by your getting married, the better you will all be able to cope with this important change in the family.

You will probably want her input and depend on her party-giving experiences to help you make many of your decisions. In many ways your mother has been waiting for this opportunity ever since you were born. It also gives her a chance to feel young again, to relive her own wedding, making this gala everything she had always wished hers had been. Who knows? Perhaps your grandmother overly directed your parents' wedding, and your mother had little say in it.

Your challenge will be to take pleasure in the process of bonding with your mother, work out your

> He that would the daughter win,
> Must with the mother first begin.

separation issues as they come up, and maintain your standing as a loving daughter who is leaving the nest. When something illuminates your divergent views and opinions about the wedding, your mother may try to convince you that you are wrong and she is right. Some mothers can become antagonistic when others refuse to conform to their ways.

What if you have one of those mothers? What could be motivating her? Just hold your ground. Such a mother is most likely driven by society's long-standing assignment to women as the people in charge of maintaining the family's emotional order. In traditional families men control economics and power, while women manage relationships. Their habit of taking charge is hard to break, and your mother will need your gentle prodding to let go. You might sigh at this point, knowing that she can be a pain in your plans!

At the same time remember that though she can be overbearing, your mother does have a wonderful eye for flowers—why not put her in charge of working with the florist? If you asked her, she might get off the subject of your partner's religion and concentrate instead on preparing driving directions for the guests. Or she could call around to find a photographer. With her beautiful handwriting, she could execute the invitations and place cards (that ought to keep her busy for a while). Get the idea?

There are countless details that you can entrust to your willing and eager mother. You really don't have to do everything by yourself—or do you? As the person on center stage, hundreds of details need your attention during this time. What about the other areas of your already hectic life, such as your job, your laundry, and your relationship? You don't have to let yourself get sucked into wedding stress.

Unless you are a perfectionist who drives herself needlessly, you really do not want to deal with every aspect of planning this celebration. It can be liberating to make this a joint family project and your mother would gain a real sense of pleasure from her participation in the painstaking effort to make your wedding beautiful.

As the prospective bride, you can benefit from your mother's assistance and support, especially if you are feeling a little disorganized or overwhelmed by the massive task before you. Don't worry about letting her have the pleasure of helping you—just continually make it clear as to what you do and do not want. There is nothing wrong with indulging her.

Keeping things in perspective is key. The issues are rarely about clashing tastes. More often in this dance

mothers and daughters go through their own personal struggles. This is really part of the "ups and downs" of the normal family development cycle. She will have to let go as you "officially" become an adult and part of a new family.

MOTHER LOSS

The issue of missing family members becomes especially relevant during these wedding planning days. When your mother is absent—whether she has abandoned you because of her death or is otherwise disassociated from your life—the old piercing pain returns fresh and raw. Dealing with the complexities of such circumstances is a challenging and necessary part of emotionally surviving during your engagement.

Connie came to see me when she was twenty-eight years old. She was worried and concerned about herself. Although she had a very good job as a paralegal, was attractive, friendly, and had many friends, she couldn't understand why none of her relationships with men ever reached the marriage level. She was at that time dating Mark, whom she really liked, and she feared this relationship would suffer a similar fate.

Connie's mother had died of cancer when she was ten years old. Connie, who had been incredibly attached to her mother, had no one to help her deal with her grief nor take her mother's place. Her father was an aloof, hardworking businessman, who hired a succession of nannies that hardly fulfilled the task. During a relaxation trance in one of our sessions, Connie had an epiphany and discovered what might have been thwarting her goal. Connie's terror of having a child who would be abandoned, as she had been by her mother, was sabotaging her conscious desire to get married and have a family.

For the next several sessions, Connie and I devised a "grief ritual" to assist her in completing the mourning process for her mother. She wrote a poem, found some photographs and a favorite necklace of her mother's, and spent some time at her mother's grave site. She "talked" to her, shared her concerns, cried for the loss of this very important person. And the healing began.

When Mark asked Connie to marry him she was ready to say yes. During the wedding planning process, Connie sorely missed her mother. The sweetness of this time was punctuated by the renewed pain of her loss. In an effort to soothe herself, Connie created her mother's presence in a myriad of ways. Deep down she knew her mother would have loved Mark, would have been thrilled that her daughter was marrying such a fine person.

Connie would often recall the image of her mother and tell her private things that she couldn't share with anyone else. Connie's mother had had excellent taste and Connie fantasized her reaction when choosing her colors, wedding dress, and the floral arrangements. Connie even included her mother's name on the wedding invitation. When her father walked her down the aisle, Connie told him how much she missed having her mother there.

Surprisingly, the usually aloof businessman wept and hugged his daughter warmly.

*K*elly was eight years old when she saw her mother drive away in a white Cadillac convertible. She and the handsome blonde man who had his arm around her were laughing so hard they never noticed the little girl peering out her bedroom window. Kelly's mom never returned and no one ever talked about it.

Eventually, her dad remarried and Kelly was introduced to her new "mom." This was a happy new family for Kelly's father, his wife, and the brothers and sisters who came along over the next ten years. Kelly was not always happy. Yet, she willed herself not to think about her mother because she had somehow gotten the idea that it would be wrong to do and she didn't want to worry her father.

Engaged and in love at twenty-six years of age, Kelly unexpectedly sank into a depression. What should have been the most blissful phase of her life turned into a dark, tearful time. Until they came to see me, Kelly and her fiancé were completely confused by this turn of events and considered canceling their marriage.

Old family issues always crop up during important family life transitions and in Kelly's case the secret of her mother's disappearance was a massive gap. The upcoming wedding loosened this bride-to-be from her strict chain of defenses regarding her terrible loss. It was unfinished business. Unfinished, because she had not had the opportunity to grieve when the loss occurred. Understanding these dynamics allowed the young couple to move forward with their wedding plans, while Kelly concurrently opened the door to let her grief out.

During their engagement, women without mothers reexperience the full sorrow of their loss. No wonder, since this is a time when a woman wants to share her happiness and needs her mother's guidance and experience. Don't be surprised if many years from now—even after you have mourned well for the woman who was your greatest ally, even if your anger about the woman who abandoned you has been resolved—you experience fresh waves of grief at your own children's weddings.

Two major issues a motherless bride faces are that she missed out on the crucial opportunity to model herself after her mother and that she needs to emotionally separate from her. How can you pattern yourself after a myth, after someone who has, even unintentionally, abandoned you? How can you model yourself after someone you hate? How can you separate from someone who has not been there? Resolving issues is a task best done with someone who is alive and available; it is

The best way to deal with family secrets is to stop keeping them. Instead, start talking with family members and ask questions.

much more difficult to work things out with a memory. More difficult, yes, but hardly impossible, as you saw with Connie, given the appropriate guidance.

One of the developmental tasks that a wedding brings to light is the work of the final reconciliation and separation between a mother and daughter. Getting married transforms a woman's childhood perspective regarding her mother and shifts their relationship to one of peers. She has her own husband now, is an adult in the full meaning of the word, and no longer needs to prove herself as her mother's equal because she is. There is also a sense of camaraderie between the two generations—the mother who has lived through this marriage ritual can now be her daughter's mentor. And the daughter can finally let go of her adolescent grievances. When a woman is motherless, she cannot experience these changes firsthand.

These are the tasks of adolescence and adulthood which a daughter needs to negotiate in order to become a psychologically whole adult. Nothing is more devastating to a child than the death of her mother. The older the child and the more loving and stable the relationship was, the greater the possibility for healing. Full recovery from such a terrible loss can never happen completely. However, it is possible that after many years the painful legacy of fear and heartache will be replaced by love and hope. If your relationship with your deceased mother was difficult or ambivalent, then I would urge you to consider counseling to help you with your leftover anger and grief.

A daughter who was physically deserted by her mother also endures a kind of death and has many similar issues. Since this form of abandonment is utterly within the category of abuse, these daughters carry the ever-present baggage of anger and rejection. With the right kind of attention, the pain of such a loss can be overcome to a great degree.

Daughters whose mothers have "emotionally" deserted them through neglect or physical or emotional abuse often exhibit many of the same problems as daughters who have lost their mothers through death or physical abandonment. However, the hope of reconnection is ever present and ever possible. And wedding plans are often just the needed catalyst for reconciliation. A competent psychotherapist can be invaluable in getting past such ordeals.

As difficult as it is to overcome the pain of bereavement, the healing process can be reestablished no matter when it was interrupted. Give yourself the opportunity to mourn now even if you believed that you were finished with grieving long ago. With every crisis in life the mourning process reemerges, giving vent to a new cycle of grief. This could be a good time to visit your mother's grave and to talk about her to those who knew her. You might want to write her a letter and imagine a response from her as well.

Brenda Lee found herself dreaming about her mother for the first time in years. With the wedding she had always wanted just weeks away, she could not understand why she felt so depressed. When we spoke about her feelings, she recognized that she felt sorry for herself. Brenda Lee's mom had died of a heart attack when she was nineteen. Though Brenda Lee's love for her mother had been intense, she had grown to love her father's new wife, Leslie.

"Leslie is a doll," said Brenda Lee. "We're really good friends and she's been such a big help to me. But lately I find myself angry at her for not being my mother."

"What in particular brings out your anger?" I asked.

"You know," she replied, "she just intrudes everywhere with her rigid opinions and if I disagree with her she inevitably gets insulted."

"What do you do then?" I countered.

"I end up feeling upset that I hurt her feelings," answered Brenda Lee, "and after a while we go on to the next thing."

"That sounds normal," I said. "What makes you think it would be any different with your mother if she were still alive?"

"Well . . ." Brenda Lee floundered, "maybe she wouldn't have been so different. When I think back to how things were when I was a teenager . . . we fought plenty!"

"Chances are," I said, "that you would have had altercations with your mother had she lived. They may have been different than these that you experience with your stepmother. Nevertheless, you miss your mother and that's natural."

Brenda Lee began by writing her mother a letter that expressed her feelings of missing her. Not surprisingly, she was soon in touch with her rage toward her natural mother, who again was absent when she needed her. Layer by layer, Brenda Lee was able to access memories of incidents she had experienced with her mother during her adolescence for which she still harbored anger, but which she had never allowed herself to express because she felt guilty about having negative feelings toward her deceased mother.

Little by little, the anger, once expressed, was replaced by intense feelings of love and connection with the woman who was lost so long ago. And then Brenda Lee wrote one more letter to her mother, where she asked her for some guidance during this tumultuous

time of her life. During a relaxation exercise, Brenda Lee had a distinct experience of attachment with the mother she had loved and lost. In the following days, some dreams reinforced her sense of being connected with her mother and soon thereafter I encouraged Brenda Lee to write another letter. I asked her to imagine what her mother might write back to her were that possible. This is what was produced.

To My Darling Daughter, Brenda Lee,

I know you are having a lot of mixed up feelings during this most important time in your life. I wanted you to know how happy I am that you found Jason. If I was picking out someone to take care of you and to love you as you deserve to be loved, I couldn't have done better. Jason and I would have loved each other and been great friends.

It's hard for a girl without her mother to guide her through some of the knotty moments that getting married brings on. I remember on my wedding day my own mother had to rescue me from my mother-in-law's interference during the ceremony. She was, as you may remember, a very difficult woman. I suppose your future mother-in-law is not the easiest person to get to know either, but lucky for you, you have Leslie and your dad, who love you so much, in your corner. I'm glad you have her. Don't blame her for acting like a mother—I doubt if everything would have run smoothly between us either. Leslie cares for you as if you were her own daughter. Let her love you, I really don't mind if you do.

My darling daughter, I am so proud of the adult you became. You were always a loving person, a giving girl, and now you have turned into a truly beautiful human being. Even though I won't be with you in person, I'll always be with you in spirit no matter what.

Luvya tons,

Kisses,

Your ever loving Mom

Without the actual presence of a mother, a daughter deals in a vacuum—unless of course she was lucky enough to have had a loving stepmother, aunt, or mentor whom she allowed to take her mother's place. If this happens, the modeling and separation issues that a woman needs to accomplish can be realized more easily and a completely healthy emotional life can be recovered. This was the case with Brenda Lee, whose relationship with her stepmother mirrored the machinations that would have taken place with her natural mother. The therapeutic work that Brenda Lee accomplished in her letter-writing helped her resolve many of her leftover feelings.

However, even in the best of circumstances there still will remain a small pocket of emptiness. Allow

LETTER-WRITING
LINK

1. On the first day, write your mother a loving letter expressing your feelings for her.

2. On the second day, allow yourself to access your anger toward the mother who is not here when you need her. Try not to be afraid to let out all your negative feelings. The positive ones will return a hundred-fold.

3. On the third day, let yourself remember incidents you experienced with your mother during your lifetime for which you felt anger or resentment. You have nothing to feel guilty about. If your mother

(continues)

yourself these normal feelings of sadness. Letting yourself experience the full range of your emotions helps you to work through the remaining grief. In time the pain will feel more and more distant, and you will be left with a tenderness for the woman who gave you life.

Many of the same issues occur if you have lost your father. Saying good-bye is the most difficult task that people who have lost either of their parents must confront. Don't be surprised if you experience a repetition of grief-related behavior, including anger and sadness for the parent who abandoned you—and don't blame yourself or feel guilty for these natural emotions during this important time in your life.

If you would like to progress in your grieving process with your mother (or father) you can utilize the steps outlined in Letter-writing Link. Letter-writing is a powerful tool. Do not rush things along. For best results only write one letter each day.

STEPMOTHERS

Your relationship with your stepmother, if you have one, is a particularly complicated one. This relationship is commonly fraught with passionate feelings of competition and jealousy. (See the discussion in Chapter 4, "If Your Parents Are Divorced.") It is helpful to keep in mind that your stepmother is in a particularly difficult position. If you are confused about how to manage your relationship with her it may be a good idea to understand her motives.

Your stepmother wants to be an important part of the family, yet does not really have a place of her own in all the wedding-related hoopla. She cannot take your mother's place, nor can she be the recipient of the honors that your mother deserves. For instance, you might not invite her to be part of the wedding party, nor would you include her name on the invitation. You cannot make it up to her if she has no children of her own, but you can show sensitivity to how much she cares for you and needs to be included as part of the family.

Many prospective brides who have friendly relations involve their stepmothers in the wedding planning process by giving them an important role and keeping them current on the particulars. You would be remiss if you did not ask her if she would like to wear your wedding colors, buy her some flowers, include her in some of the photography sessions, and ask your fiancé to be sure to save her a dance.

On the other hand, if you are close to your stepmother because she raised you—regardless of whether your mother is involved or not—then she could have a prominent role in the wedding planning and may

were alive, she would be encouraging you to spit out the negative feelings you have toward her so that you could let them go.

4. On the fourth day, write one more letter to your mother and ask her for guidance during this tumultuous time.

5. On the fifth day, achieve a relaxation state utilizing any method you are familiar with. Decide in advance to feel a connection with your mother—you may want to take out a photograph to help you. Now write another letter addressed to you from your own mother. Just let go and allow your imagination free reign.

deserve to be treated by you and everyone else as if she were your mother. In some cases both mothers could get equal treatment. Some women consider following such a course when they realize that their stepmother treated them like her own daughter, and now it is time for them to treat their stepmother like a real mother.

As with all of your other relationships, do not be surprised if some old issues come flying out of the proverbial closet. This is a good time to mend unresolved problems. Your challenge will be to remain sensitive to your stepmother even while your emotional connection with your mother is at its height. Interestingly, because men are generally less involved with the work of emotional relationships, stepfathers are usually far more easily absorbed into their stepchildren's lives. In most cases, they allow their wives to freely negotiate with the children.

YOUR SECOND TIME AROUND

> We can complain because rose bushes have thorns or rejoice because thorn bushes have roses.
>
> DAG HAMMERJOLD

ℋaving been down the prenuptial road once rarely makes the journey any easier the next time. Actually, the complications of second, third, and fourth marriages can be formidable for all participants. Even if you are careful, past entanglements can turn your wedding world into something of a soap opera. Everyone from ex-spouses on one or both sides, to children, stepchildren, stepparents, former in-laws, future in-laws, and friends—not to mention your family of origin—can get caught in the web.

The wedding process by its very nature shakes up the emotional fabric of your life more than you have ever imagined. Added to the normal complications involved in getting married in the first place (as cited in previous chapters), you are dealing with the leftover grief surrounding the loss of a prior marriage, whether that marital experience ended in divorce or the death of a spouse. (Not to mention the traumatic divorce experience itself, which becomes another crucial issue for reflection and resolution.) Children from previous marriages create further ambiguity regarding family membership and loyalty and are a constant reminder of the loss that preceded the union you are now contemplating.

While getting married for the first time entails combining two families, subsequent marriages can involve three or more family constellations. As a bride-to-be for the second time around, or if you are marrying someone who has been previously wed, you must come to terms with your preceding pain, or his, and with more baggage than you might have thought you would be facing at this time.

SOME CHALLENGES AND SOLUTIONS

Often, couples facing their second time around face similar issues. While it may seem that you are the only person who has ever gone through this chaos, take heart, and remember the following tips.

Most women want and deserve to be the primary love object for their husbands. The challenge for the remarried couple is that former spouses and children from previous marriages often induce feelings of guilt and ambivalence. *Solution:* Prepare to be patient as the complicated emotions work themselves out over time. At the same time, negotiate for your right to be number one in his life.

Newlyweds have a host of issues to deal with that bridge the state of singlehood and matrimony. The challenge for the remarried couple is that in addition to those pressures, other complex structures impact the couple and in turn influence the new marriage. *Solution:* When you and your spouse are temporarily sidetracked from your marriage by children or former family members, find it in your heart to be understanding. Find creative means to meet your needs.

Most young couples have the luxury of time and emotional space to cement their union. When children are involved the couple is challenged to find time and energy to promote the efficacy of their relationship. *Solution:* Although you will have less alone time with your partner, remember that it is quality that counts. You and your spouse deserve at least one night a week, one weekend a month, and two weeks a year alone, uninterrupted by outsiders. Don't settle for less!

Disparate expectations regarding marriage are more prevalent in a couple when one has been previously wed and the other has not. The single spouse often underestimates the degree to which his or her partner's former marriage will influence the new relationship. The formerly married spouse may expect security, stability and a full family life, while the never-married spouse may expect exclusivity and romance. *Solution:* Communicate with each other about what each of you envisions to be marital bliss. You may discover similarities and differences, and can arrange for compromises and revisions.

First marriages generally fall into a relatively beneficial marital arrangement of responsibilities and provisions, and a minimal amount of negotiation may be necessary. The challenge for the remarried couple is to reach a point where the reciprocal aspect of the marriage is highlighted. *Solution:* Spell out what each partner expects to receive from and give to the other spouse. Address all areas of family life, including sex, children, in-laws, power, money, time together and apart, and household responsibilities.

BE PREPARED FOR PEYTON PLACE

Be prepared for chaos, conflict, and confusion. Apart from settling family relationships, you will also be dealing with who gets invited and who does not. Who pays for what? Who walks down the aisle and in what order? Who stands up with the bride and groom? Where do you seat the various families without slighting anyone? Then you have the sticky problem of how to handle the fragile wedding day emotions of children (regardless of their age) from a former marriage.

Finally, don't forget about your partner. What if he cannot cope with the Peyton Place atmosphere or the possible hostility from friends and family? Encourage him to be patient, be extra sensitive to his trials, and don't hesitate to enter counseling together for a little while. When both parties are willing there are always solutions.

*W*hen Abby Katz decided to marry Victor Rivers she kept her last name for the sake of her son, Russell. Russell's father had died when he was nine years old, and Russell worried that if Abby became a "Rivers" she would no longer be his mother. Victor was a flexible man and completely understood her reason for abandoning tradition.

When Victor's father got wind of this decision he was livid. How he carried on! He moaned, screamed, cursed, and put pressure on Victor until Victor begged Abby to reconsider in order to placate his father. But Abby refused to be dictated to, resented her future father-in-law, was shocked at his behavior, and held firm. That was only the beginning.

Two hours before the ceremony, Mr. Rivers telephoned saying that he refused to attend the wedding unless his son assured him that his new wife would take on the family name. Victor fought with his father, who was merciless. He again begged Abby to change her name for the sake of family peace. Abby was enraged at her fiancé's inability to handle his father and insisted he begin acting like an adult and stand up to him even if it meant that his father would miss the wedding.

Victor was very upset, but realized that he owed his allegiance to his bride-to-be. And besides, though his father's attitude was based on tradition, it was quite inappropriate considering that he had already carefully explained his and Abby's reasons.

An hour before the ceremony Victor called his father and said, "Dad, it hurts me deeply that you are acting this way. Abby gets to choose the name she will use. Of course I want you to be at my wedding, but it is completely your choice."

Victor's father and mother both attended the wedding.

Victor persevered and deserved credit for standing up to his father. What saved their marriage, let alone their wedding day, however, was Abby's courage to be loyal to her own needs and to be appropriately forthcoming with her anger at Victor for his inability to firmly set boundaries with his father. Yes, I did say courage! It is not easy to rock the boat, especially in the thrust of such a beautiful life event as getting married. It takes the emotional corollary to getting into a glacial pool of water: You just take a deep breath, hold your nose, and jump!

Interestingly, Victor, Abby, and Russell's story had a particularly happy ending. Two years after the wedding Russell proposed that Victor adopt him, and both Russell and his mother legally change their names to Rivers so that they could be one big happy family. At the adoption ceremony that the family created, Victor's parents were thrilled witnesses as they became proud grandparents.

In this time of joyful crisis expect that some catastrophe will take place. The more complicated the family dynamics, the more room there is for mishaps. By anticipating a calamity, you can develop protection for your delicate psyche and solutions to get your forthcoming marriage on the right track. One task my clients find helpful is to script out some possible trouble spots in advance. You know who all the players are. Let your imagination run wild. Worst case scenario, what could happen?

If this is your first marriage and your fiancé's second, try not to get yourself too upset about his indifference to

MARGARET'S LIST OF POTENTIAL PITFALLS

Here is the list that this bride made a week prior to her second marriage. The check marks reflect the situations that subsequently took place.

- My daughter will have a fight with her boyfriend and won't show up at the wedding.
- √ My fiancé's former wife will call him on some pretext and get him upset.
- My former husband will call crying to my

(continues)

wedding details. Having been to the altar once may have dampened his mild male enthusiasm for wedding hoopla. Should you submerge your own dream wedding? Absolutely not! In the face of a less than enthusiastic groom your best bet is to take a realistic stance: It is your first and last time to walk down the aisle with the man you adore—make your special day everything you ever fantasized. Despite his lukewarm demeanor before the ceremony, your fiancé will come to life when he says "I do."

Why might he be so unenthusiastic? Ask him. (Don't forget to take another look at Chapter 3, which describes men's general apathy to wedding festivities.) Previously married men have the added burden of feeling embarrassed to have failed the first time. Perhaps your fiancé worries that his kids will be upset witnessing an all-out spectacle. (Well, you did fall in love with him because of his sensitivity.) Whatever the cause of his reluctance to have a gala, try to realize that this has little, if anything, to do with you—it's not because he loves you any less. Instead, let him know calmly, lovingly, and assertively that this is a once-in-a-lifetime event for you and *you really need his help* to make it beautiful for both of you.

If this is your second time around and his virgin flight, be sure to take his needs into consideration.

Chances are he will expect you to take the lead anyway. It will be up to you to decide if you wish to wear a pastel suit or a traditional white wedding gown. There are no rules except to please yourself and your partner.

Should former spouses be invited to the wedding? Can you maintain friendships with them and still look forward to marital bliss with spouse number two? Is there room for a new marriage when the former one is still alive? How do you deal with your groom's ex-wife? Can your new spouse be expected to befriend your ex?

The best policy is to keep in mind the old adage, "off with the old and on with the new." There is *no* room at your wedding or in your life for any ex's—they are part of the past and should stay there. Emotionally completing the divorce process is a crucial step in paving the way for a successful new marriage. If you feel badly about hurting your kids by turning your back on their father, it's too late. It is also in their best interest to face the reality of their parents' divorce—you will both always be their parents, but the marriage is over.

mother that she should try to stop the wedding.

√ My father, who can't handle change, will get sick and end up in the hospital.

• My future stepdaughter will pout throughout the day.

• People will compare everything to my first wedding.

• I'll break down and wish I was still married to my first husband.

√ My future stepson will wear something totally inappropriate.

BLENDING FAMILIES

What about the *Brady Bunch* phenomenon? Do you really expect it can happen? Can your children, or his

for that matter, be expected to become an instant family with you? Naturally, you would like nothing better than to be one big happy family.

In reality this rarely happens unless you enter each other's families when the children are very young, or if their biological parent is deceased. It is useful to understand what goes into shaping children's feelings. Children have no control over what happens to them and have not asked that their parents divorce or die, nor remarry. Most crucial is the knowledge that children of divorce usually feel angry about the dissolution of their family, and will irrationally blame a new stepparent for killing the fantasy of their parents' reconciliation.

Even when children are prepared for a parent's remarriage they are agitated by the event. Most experience a very powerful sense of divided loyalty that interferes with their ability to feel kindly toward their new stepparent. As a newlywed with stepchildren, you can accomplish a great deal by not taking hurtful actions and words personally. This requires your ability to put yourself in your stepchildren's shoes, and to harness inner power and outer supports.

What matters most, however, is that you and your new spouse are the ones who come first now, and the burden rests squarely on both of you to be responsible for these new relations. It takes communication, sensitivity, and lots of patience—and sometimes even that cannot produce total harmony between all parties. But if you wait long enough, miracles can happen.

PRENUPTIALS AND POSTNUPTIALS

An issue that is most frequently found in second marriages is the sensitive one of signing a prenuptial agreement, a contract that defines who gets what if a marriage falls apart. Most people think about it, many discuss it, and a growing number of both first and second marriages have one. What do you do if after the love of your life proposes, he springs another kind of proposal on you, saying, "Listen, sweetheart, I've spoken to my lawyer and . . . look it's really no big deal . . . but she's drawing up a prenuptial agreement and I'd like you to sign it."

Prenuptials can be full of thorns. After all, their implicit message is that the marriage may not succeed or that the partners do not trust one another. When the subject comes up, some prospective brides feel so shocked they consider canceling their wedding. After all, they wonder, "If he doesn't trust me why get married?" But, male or female, if you own a business, are

**THINKING ABOUT
PRENUPTIAL
AGREEMENTS**

1. *What if you are the
   one reluctant to enter
   a prenuptial proposal?*
   Initially you may
   find the idea of a
   prenuptial agreement
   repugnant. Allow
   yourself some time to
   think things over
   before you react.
   Inquire as to his rea-
   sons for asking for
   this. Just listen, suspend judgment, and
   try putting yourself in
   his place. One of the
   most important things
   to consider is whether
   your fiancé's motiva-
   tion is reasonable.

2. *How do you tell if your
   partner has a genuine
   need to protect himself?*

   (continues)

wealthy, divorced, or have children from a previous marriage, lawyers recommend the practice as a prudent one. In addition, business partners often pressure each other to sign prenuptial contracts to protect the business from potential matrimonial involvement.

*L*eslie was extremely annoyed when her fiancé, Ben, suggested a prenuptial agreement. "Do you think I'm out to get your money, you jerk? I've got my own damn money!" she hollered.

Ben tried to calm her down, reasoning that her past marriage and his (they each had two children), combined with their lucrative medical practices, made a prenuptial a smart idea. Leslie refused to speak with Ben about the subject, or any other, for nearly a month. Finally she did some research, talked to her lawyer, some friends, and a fellow physician, all of whom agreed that a prenuptial was wise. It actually protected them both in a variety of ways.

Slowly the two hammered out the terms, stipulating that a portion of their incomes be combined for living expenses and savings, and a portion be set aside for each of their children, their parents, and for reinvestment in their practices. After several happy years of marriage, Ben and Leslie combined their medical practices and their bank accounts with no mixed emotions.

Though initially antagonistic to her fiancé's pragmatic approach, Leslie was too smart to let her emotions rule. Certainly it first seemed to her that Ben did not trust her or the institution of marriage. Separating love and logic is not easy during this supposedly romantic period. It takes a mature person like Leslie to put romance and hurt feelings aside and deal with practical matters like these.

Prenuptials can also spell out marital responsibilities. For instance, a common scenario is one in which a woman helps her husband through medical school and contractually obligates him to reciprocate in kind. He agrees that down the road he will put her through school, too. Only you and your lawyer can decide if a prenuptial agreement is sensible and appropriate for you. You might consider the three points in Thinking About Prenuptial Agreements.

Another choice, a novel approach that I think of as a *postnuptial agreement,* is based on a modicum of trust but can greatly alleviate prenuptial jitters. This is a method I devised for Paula and Lenny when they got married.

Although they were in accord regarding the need for a contract, they just could not come to terms on many of the details. Paula and Lenny fought bitterly in the lawyer's office.

Paula said, "It seemed as if we were working out a divorce, rather than a marriage. Our engagement was in jeopardy."

Ask yourself if there are integrity and common sense in the provisions he has requested. Are you comfortable complying with his requirements? Get legal advice. Try to be objective about his commitment to you. You have been confident until now that this relationship was genuinely good for you; do note that nothing personal has changed. It may be a good time to seek guidance from a psychotherapist.

3. Supposing you are the instigator and are met by objections from your partner. What can you do?

   Try to reassure him of your love and ask

(continues)

him to take some time and suspend his decision. When he is in a calm frame of mind, ask him to listen and not interrupt as you list your purpose and rationale. Throughout, remind him about your commitment to him, citing examples to back this up. When you are done, be quiet and available to actively listen to his feelings. Validate his response and offer some compromises. Should there be differences, you could seek additional legal counsel to iron out the disparities.

Lenny related, "Things were starting to get ugly between us. I was ready to call off the wedding."

Happily, Paula and Lenny decided to get a different kind of counsel and came to me. I suggested postponing the process until after their honeymoon. It took a giant leap of faith for Paula and Lenny to follow their intuition—but isn't that what marriage is about anyway? What a tremendous relief to be able to let go of this issue and get on with the wedding and with life together.

About a month after returning from their wedding trip, Paula and Lenny executed their postnuptial contract with ease. What made the difference was that they were now more strongly motivated to be fair to each other and to work things out successfully. Sometimes the idea of a postnuptial contract is frightening, yet it can work out to be a blessing.

COLD FEET AND OTHER JITTERS

Kindness in words creates confidence. Kindness in thinking creates profoundness. Kindness in giving creates love.

LAO-TSE

*W*hether it began with a meeting of eyes across a crowded room, or answering a personal ad, or sharing a laugh with the stranger next to you at the movies, or bumping into a car as you backed out of a parking space, or cheering together as Phil Simms threw a touchdown pass, all it took was one spark to start your forest fire! Your search has ended. You have made the promise and your wedding bells are imminent. And yet, the very thing we wish for so fervently—to be coupled, to be engaged, to be married happily ever after—we also fear. The idea of marriage can be both frightening and thrilling, like walking a tightrope over the Grand Canyon.

*T*aking off her make-up one night—just two weeks before her wedding—Lois looked at her tearful eyes in the mirror and questioned herself for the umpteenth time.

Lois: So what is with you?

Lois in the mirror (LM): I feel rotten, didn't sleep all night.

Lois: Better get yourself in shape, girl, you need all your wits about you. Work's never been more important, you gotta make those sales today. And then there's all the wedding stuff. Yikes!!!

LM: I know, I know, don't pressure me.

Lois: It's the quota, you gotta meet the quota, or else how are you going to be successful?

LM: Don't I know it! Maybe we're making a mistake. It is really too much pressure. I'm not ready to be a grown-up.

Lois: What are you talking about? You're thirty-one years old. It's about time you got married and had a husband, kids, the whole deal.

LM: Kids, I hate kids. Did you ever know any kids you liked?

Lois: You know what they say, your own are different.

LM: I want out! I'm too young, I'm not ready to be a mother, let alone a wife. And besides, have you ever known anyone who's had a good marriage?

Lois: Lois, don't be a jerk! Les is different. You love him. He loves you. You have so much in common, he really turns you on, you have fun together. It'll be great!

LM: But what if it's not? What do I do then? I'll be trapped forever. What if he turns into his father? Or worse yet, my father!

Is it any wonder that brides like Lois go through such turmoil? These are some of the inevitable last minute worries that you have to deal with when you are mar-riage-bound. Despite lifelong anticipation and excite-ment, prospective brides nevertheless experience waves of uneasiness or ambivalence. True, you have decided, but how can you be sure? And you thought only men had second thoughts.

The unpredictable creates feelings of discomfort, insecurity, and fear—that is normal. "What changes?" you may wonder. Perhaps you find yourself thinking, "We are in love, we are perfect for each other, we have a great relationship, marriage won't be any different—and yet I'm nervous." Don't worry, you are normal. A number of things do shift in your life. Once married you become each other's family and the commitment becomes surprisingly stronger once it is permanent. Marriage is so reassuring that most women find that they can relax as they create a new beginning.

A good part of your ambivalence is probably based on the differences between you and your fiancé regard-ing the forthcoming gala. The wedding details that are swirling around your head all night only seem to annoy your one and only. You begin to wonder if he really loves you and if getting married is really important to him. It is hard to remember that most men have little interest in the hundreds of fine points that need atten-tion to successfully bring a wedding to fruition. Your

As the wedding day nears, the unpredictability of marriage often creates a sense of discomfort, insecurity, and fear—this is to be expected.

obsession with wedding details is not a sign of early psychosis but merely an out-of-control fervor designed to make it all turn out perfectly.

Not surprisingly, the pressure of planning a wedding ignites conflict over issues that are irrelevant as well as significant to your relationship with your future spouse. The different degrees of intensity with which you and your fiancé approach wedding planning are really not a measure of whether you will have a good marriage. On the other hand, most engaged couples quarrel over some basic topics that are rather important. These usually include the issues of time, money, religion, family, wedding politics, and sex. Despite the toxicity that these topics can provoke, you both need to reach a mutual understanding.

OVERCOMING PRE-WEDDING FEARS

Considering that the road to the altar and beyond is filled with unseen obstacles and setbacks, it is quite healthy to have some fears and doubts about marriage. Soon-to-be brides and their grooms tend to experience some of the following feelings of ambivalence at some point before their wedding date:

I am not ready to get married. Perhaps you feel fearful about settling down and losing your identity, or you don't feel mature enough to get married. It is not as much the man you are marrying as the *idea* of being married that scares you. Try imagining yourself single again—in great detail. Do not envision just the good parts either; recall the loneliness and frustrations as well. Perhaps singlehood isn't all you are romanticizing it to be.

I am worried about finances. If you are like most brides, you are concerned about how you and your fiancé will handle your finances in the future. Should you continue to keep your money separate, except for a "family fund"? Many couples do. Do you give up total control of your economic freedom to your future husband? This is the traditional approach. Yet, there is a way to join fiscally and still maintain a sense of autonomy.

If you choose to keep funds separate will your marriage be any less successful? The answer is no. In these modern times men and women can maintain a loving connection without being joined at the financial hip. But how should you and your fiancé determine what is best for the two of you? As difficult as these issues are, you must confront the topic

of money—do not take the coward's way out by sweeping it under the rug.

I am scared about losing my economic freedom. Women often worry about becoming dependent or a burden on their partner—especially after children if they plan to stop working. Talk things over with your fiancé if you are plagued by this fear. You will reach a shared understanding and, with open communication about financial independence, you can create some interesting solutions. Some of the women I've worked with created a "baby fund" after their wedding—a special bank account into which they made monthly deposits to effect a modicum of financial independence after they gave birth.

I don't think I will be a good spouse or parent. Odds are you come from a somewhat dysfunctional family yourself (as do about two-thirds of your peers) and you are naturally concerned about repeating unhealthy relationships with your own spouse and children. Recognizing the magnitude of being a good wife and mother is half the battle.

Your consciousness is already raised, therefore you are going to make better choices than your parents. Be on the lookout for the repetition of harmful patterns of communication and stop them early. Keep in mind that if you run into any serious problems along the way professional counseling is always available. All that is left is to listen, talk, and be loving—and you will probably succeed with flying colors.

I don't like being the center of attention. Weddings can turn even the most relaxed and self-assured people into a bundle of nerves. You are a princess for a day, the subject of nearly every photograph and the talk on everyone's lips. This is your own mini Broadway show. Remember that you can tailor your wedding to your own specifications. You do not have to include traditions that feel uncomfortable—for example, sit with your friends instead of separately at a dais. Make an effort to relax and keep the formalities only to the extent you are comfortable with them.

This wedding has gotten totally out of control. Guess what, all weddings do. Think about some of the pleasant aspects of your upcoming wedding and of spending the rest of your life with the man you love. If you have serious reservations about specific wedding details, by all means take control and do something. But if you are just feeling dizzy about the whole thing, take a deep breath and think about the honeymoon. Remember, it is just a five-hour party; your guests will have a good time and so will you.

Life will become predictable and dull. During courtship, whether or not people live together, a certain amount of excitement is tied to the uncertainty of the relationship. Once a state of permanence is established, the previous doubt is replaced by assurance and security. But that does not necessarily result in complacency. Dull people create dull marriages. It is the responsibility of each partner to keep himself and herself interesting, to inject periodic excitement into the relationship by taking risks both sexually and emotionally.

I'm worried about disappointing my partner. You feel like the pressure is really on—as if you are pinned under a microscope. You are sure that everyone, including your future husband, is evaluating your personality, your looks, your career, your background, and your potential—and you are afraid that you may not measure up. Wedding-day jitters are eroding your self-confidence. We only fail when we think we are going to fail, right? He is marrying you because he loves you. Ask him for reassurance, talk about your feelings, and soon you will feel comfortable and reassured. Your future happiness will evolve naturally.

I'll never be able to have sex with anyone else again. Both men and women experience regret and grief at the thought of losing their sexual independence when they marry. They mourn the loss of their freedom to flirt, seduce, and sleep with other partners. No more first kisses, no more mysterious, lusty nights! Go ahead, let yourself feel the loss. You need to say good-bye to that part of your life, and good-byes are never easy.

Individuals who admit to this fear are expressing a sentiment based on the finality and permanence of this step, which can indeed be intimidating. Although it is true that you give up variety with marriage, your sexual satisfaction can flourish. Monogamy gives us the opportunity to expand the *depth* of freedom. Imagine the possibilities between two people who trust each other fully and are able to risk complete vulnerability with each other. In addition, since much of sex is between the ears, the quality of your relationship has a direct bearing upon your sexual desire and satisfaction. Marriage

> Most brides report decreased sexual activity during the post-engagement period. Not surprisingly, both men and women suffer from a diminishment in libido during this hectic time.

is a wonderful journey that can provide you with fresh, exciting, and lusty passion.

I'm afraid of losing my independence forever. This is another common fear among women who have observed "traditional" marriages. Brides worry that their future spouse will control all their free time and keep them from seeing friends and pursuing hobbies. They assume that being married means being captured, requiring total togetherness and generally becoming "one."

Since one plus one equals two, rather than one, there is true reason to be concerned. There is a big difference between "tying the knot" and "becoming one." I once asked a woman I know what she thought about having dinner with me "one day next week" and she responded, "I don't know what I think, my husband isn't here." This person has given herself up to her spouse and has lost her "self" in the marriage—with only one "self" that marriage is operating at a great deficit.

In a viable marriage, interdependency develops between the couple—a healthy balance of independence and dependence made up of two whole individuals. Today couples negotiate their marriages differently than in the past. Men and women want relationships that offer security but also plenty of space for separateness where tolerance for each partner's personal development has the same weight as their joint interests.

I'm afraid that my partner will change after he says, "I do." You fear that the loving, kind, and considerate person that you have fallen in love with might change into a domineering or demanding monster. Understandably, poor role models may be responsible for a pessimistic attitude toward marriage. A good relationship is maintained by keeping the lines of communication free and clear. Give each other honest feedback when you feel good as well as when you are upset or unhappy.

I worry that marital responsibility will be too difficult to bear. Fearing responsibility is a lot like facing the difficult reality of growing up. It is sometimes a struggle to be a reliable, stable, and dependable adult—but along with the responsibilities you also gain a marvelous joy that only marriage brings.

Before you hit the turbulent white-water phase of wedding planning, it pays to sit down with your partner and share your feelings of ambivalence, which are

bound to come up as you paddle your way down the river toward marital bliss.

DETERMINING CONFIDENCE

Think of it this way. You are dealing with three separate entities when you get married. The first is your relationship as a couple. The second and third are the relationships each of you has with yourself. This gives you a grand total of three sources from which to draw for an abundance of stimulation, romance, and the good life.

Ruth and Harry came to see me two months before their wedding day. Ruth had many questions. Primarily she worried that she would not be happy marrying a man outside of her race. Initially, Ruth's parents and girlfriends had been totally against Harry.

"Listen," her best friend, Shelly, had remonstrated, "what's wrong with our men? You're opening up a coffin of grief, and you'll be sorry when you find yourself smack in the middle of lots of trouble."

"Ruth," her father begged, "don't rush into a decision you might regret. You do not know these people; you will never be accepted."

I asked Ruth, "What made you decide to marry Harry in the first place?"

"Harry's the first man I ever met who is truly a grown-up. When we disagree, he talks to me. He doesn't yell, he doesn't shut me out, he listens, asks questions, and keeps an open mind. He's never afraid to change his mind, admit being wrong, or insist on his own viewpoint when he thinks he's right. I respect his mind, adore his body, and love him completely as he does me. I think we could be happy together."

"Now tell me," I continued, "what are the doubts that you have?"

"It sounds disloyal to Harry," Ruth responded, "but I worry about how we'll make out as a biracial couple. I realize that society as a whole will be against us, and we'll have to forge a place for ourselves in a community that accepts mixing. And I'm nervous about going against my family and Harry's family."

"Marriage is a difficult undertaking," I said. "The more common ground there is between a couple, the more harmonious the relationship in the long run. There are always obstacles in the form of differences between people. It is a question of whether you have confidence in you and Harry as a team, and if you have honestly examined potential solutions.

Harry asked, "We've been over this ground hundreds of times way before we decided to get married. Why is Ruth feeling so uncertain now when the plans have all been finalized and the wedding is around the corner?"

"It becomes more of a reality as you inch closer to your wedding date," I responded. "Fears that had been seemingly resolved emerge again."

MENTAL REHEARSAL

1. Go ahead, allow your-self to mentally call off the engagement.
2. In your mind's eye, go through the motions of breaking the news to your partner and imagine his reaction and your own reac-tion in response.
3. What reasons would you give?
4. Is there anything he could say that would change your mind? Say it to yourself and notice your reply.
5. Now envision telling your parents, cancel-ing the reception, and informing your friends

(continues)

I taught Ruth to use the technique outlined in Mental Rehearsal to assist her in making her difficult decision.

Ruth mentally rehearsed calling off the wedding and discovered that she did not want to end her relationship with Harry. We explored the issues of race, family loy-alty, and what it means to be an independent adult. We examined the strengths within their relationship, as well as Ruth's level of courage to face potential pitfalls and solutions. Ruth concluded that they were both mature enough to overcome the problems down the road.

Most people feel somewhat nervous about tying the knot. Indeed, it is a major life change and each step in the Family Life Progression brings with it feelings of uncertainty. When we acknowledge the fear, accept it, and allow for it, we can get past it as we acknowledge its wisdom.

THE WORK OF RELATIONSHIPS

Either consciously or unconsciously many couples shy away from disturbing relationship concerns that emerge during their engagement. They foolishly believe the cul-tural myth that everything should always be exciting and joyous in a good relationship.

When a particularly significant topic causes con-tention, most people experience anxiety. There is an understandable fear caused by uncertainty about a partner's reaction. What if he disagrees, feels hurt or rejected, disapproves, gets angry, or withdraws from you? Your partner's temporary withdrawal can feel like rejection and leave you emotionally disconnected from him. Some would-be brides go so far as to consider calling off their engagement at such a juncture.

This would be a great mistake because wedding-related conflicts and doubts afford a new couple important opportunities to learn problem-solving skills, tolerate distance, and restore interrupted intimacy. Differences really do exist between people. Keep in mind that your partner is opening himself up to you when he reveals his disagreeable inner feelings, despite the pain you might feel. Do not close the door to sharing yourselves with each other. The tough part is to learn how to draw on your own inner resources when faced with the unavoidable unpleasantness that is part of the natural process of developing a good marriage.

Once you have committed to the future, you also feel a greater sense of investment in making it work. Gone will be the days when you had an "out." You will no longer find yourself wondering if he is the right one for you; that decision will have been made. Differences being what they are, you and your future husband will have many disagreements and experience occasional ill

and relatives. How does it feel? Are you relieved? Miserable? Still ambivalent? Just embarrassed?

6. Next, process all the emotional feedback you have just collected and determine what it means and what to do.

7. You will probably realize that you and your partner have decided to move forward for the right reasons. Having considered the alternative, however, you can now get back on the path to marital bliss with confidence.

feelings toward one another for the rest of your lives. What is required of both of you is a willingness to exert whatever effort it takes to see things through when conflict arises.

"Working" on your marriage—which means talking about what you like and what you don't like; standing up for what you want and don't want; and knowing when *to agree to disagree*—will protect the warm glow and loving feelings between you. When your relationship is honest, your needs get met and you are content; miraculously, there is also no desire for other sexual partners. In addition, you ought to accept the idea that you cannot possibly fulfill *all* of each other's needs. By giving each other the space to fulfill some of your individual needs elsewhere, you will have the opportunity to create a sense of freedom and satisfaction for both of you.

When we trust our ability to survive on our own, we can choose to have others in our life because we prefer the quality of those relationships—not because we need them. Although the feelings of distance that ebb and flow throughout the life of a healthy relationship may not feel good, they do not signal the end of the relationship. Rather, they provide the fodder to grow creatively as individuals.

Left to our own devices, we survive surprisingly well. Relationships rarely end when honest differences are expressed. On the contrary, we are our own worst enemy when we fail to clearly communicate honest feelings, emotions, and thoughts—in their place we store resentment and anger that tear the delicate fabric of love.

Those about to get married are suddenly catapulted into genuine adulthood regardless of how young or old they are. Responsibility and permanency are thrust upon them, seemingly with no way out. This is the basis for the fears that cause conflicts among many engaged couples (and not whether Aunt Mildred sits next to Grandpa Joe). Marriage and adulthood are riddled with doubts and insecurities. Each person, in his or her own way, comes to terms with this phenomenon. Let's take a look at an issue that engaged couples "argue around" while on their way to the altar.

As their wedding day neared, Lorraine's state of anxiety elevated. She could not sleep nights, could not concentrate on her job at the bank, had a sudden case of acne at the age of thirty-three, fought with Dean over the least little thing, lost her interest in sex, and began to doubt her choice in a husband. She felt like a total mess! Her biggest problem was that she was not sure why all this conflict was going on or what to do about it.

Lorraine had been the one who wanted to get married, although they had only known each other six months. Here it was another nine months later, the bells were about to chime, and she felt like jumping out of her skin. A dream brought her to see me.

"I woke up screaming and the sheets were soaked," Lorraine related the one time we met. "All I remember is that I was in one of those medieval dungeons like you see in the movies somewhere in Spain . . . apparently I committed some terrible crime like stealing some woman's cow. Anyway, the king held me in this wet, cold, dark room. My wrists chained in these rusty metal bracelets and I was hung on the wall on some kind of a big hook. I think I felt scared, hungry, and I had to pee . . . it was awful! It felt like I'd be there forever and there was no way out."

After I explained that almost everyone experiences ambivalence when getting married, Lorraine realized that her dream was a metaphor for the fear she felt regarding the institution of marriage. She also understood that the silly arguments she had been having with Dean had very little to do with her attachment to a particular point of view regarding a wedding detail. Rather, it was her way of attempting to take decisive control even if it was over something insignificant. Lorraine felt out of control because her life after the wedding was unknown. I suggested that she share her feelings with her fiancé and not be surprised when she discovered that he suffered from similar fears. She did. And he did. And they both felt better and more in love than ever.

No one can be absolutely certain about anything except the continuation of birth and death. Every decision involves a choice and every choice excludes another option that we have determined not to take. For Lorraine, deciding to marry Dean involved a choice that excluded the possibility of marrying someone else. Since no one has a crystal ball we cannot have a total sense of ease with any path we take. The only thing any of us can hope for is to make the best possible decision at any given point in time and accept our discomfort concerning an unpredictable future.

Marriage is no harder or easier than being single; it is just another option. A successful relationship depends on both partners' willingness to confront issues with self and other and always remembering that you are a team.

SURVIVING AMBIVALENCE

Since no one in life is perfect, you have probably decided to marry your fiancé despite the fact that he is a real flesh and blood human being with both positive and negative characteristics. Having assessed that your fiancé's personality traits make a suitable package for you, you would be wise to embrace your commitment. Naturally, you recognize that you have your own set of faults, too. But as your wedding day approaches you may have gnawing worries regarding your partner's liabilities and find yourself wondering if you will really be able to get used to them.

Martha had fallen head over heels in love with John. She had accepted his proposal eight months after they met because he was almost everything she wanted in a man. He was stable and mature, he loved her, he had a great sense of humor, he was gentle and kind, they wanted the same things from life, and they had a lot of fun together.

"Not bad," she announced to me during one of our sessions, "his only drawback is that he doesn't make much money and doesn't seem to have much desire to ever make any in the future."

Real love is not about never saying you are sorry, but rather about learning to accept and appreciate all aspects of your future husband—not just his superior qualities. Martha was confident that she would be able to adjust to a lower standard of living than she had enjoyed with her parents and expected to make up for the difference by getting a part-time job of her own. She walked down the aisle a glowing, beautiful bride. Martha and John worked hard on their marriage, and they lived happily ever after (most of the time).

DOWN THE AISLE

Marriage should be no prison, but a garden in which something higher is cultivated. . . . Marriage is something large. It is a large thing to always be two, to remain in love. . . . Wedlock is sacred.

IRVIN YALOM

Congratulations. You have made it through the turbulent period of the engagement and today is your wedding day. The bash starts in less than an hour and you are feeling panicky. You are trying to get dressed, yet people keep popping in to ask questions. Your father is more nervous than you are. You have butterflies in your stomach and your hands are literally shaking. How are you going to get through this day?

You have often wondered just how you will react. Will you be nervous? Will you cry? Will you enjoy your wedding? Will you feel happy or just numb? And now you are having all of these feelings at once. It is no wonder this day will change you forever. It is the biggest, most elaborate party you will ever throw—and you and your groom are the center of attention.

Sometimes it is hard to stay focused on the reason for all the prenuptial fuss, but try to remember that the goal of all this hoopla is simply to unite two like-minded individuals in marriage.

Next to the birth of a child, most people rank their wedding day as the happiest day of their lives. My goal is to encourage you to truly experience its joy—to engrave every delightful aspect of it in your memory. If you allow yourself to savor it, the depth of emotion you can feel on this day is limitless.

A wedding photographer once told me that he never misses the opportunity to take a picture of the newly married couple as they leave the altar and walk back down the aisle arm in arm. "You will never see two people happier than at that very moment," he observed. In the same way a photographer captures it on film, I urge you to capture the joy of your wedding in your heart and mind. Experience the here and now. Because today is unlike any other day in your life, let it be etched in your memory forever.

Oh, no! It has started to drizzle. Do not despair—rain is something even the most organized bride has no control over. In addition to the weather, plenty of other little things can go wrong on your wedding day. The flowers could be late . . . your mother could get a panic

attack . . . the printed directions could turn out wrong
. . . the fathers could have a disagreement over money . . .
you could have a bad hair day . . . the best man could be
hung over . . . the band could be awful . . . Uncle Sylvester
could make a scene. . . . What can you do?

Wedding-day disasters vary from mild to cata-
strophic. Chances are pretty good that your experience
will fall somewhere in the middle of the spectrum.
Hopefully you have anticipated a problem or two so
that when a disaster occurs you will be able to deal with
it. More than likely you will experience a modicum of
anxiety anyway, and the unavoidable mishaps will feel
a little upsetting. But you do not have to allow anyone
or anything to spoil your special day. Take a deep
breath and try the exercise in Putting Things in
Perspective if you are struck by an unfortunate incident.

> ### PUTTING THINGS IN PERSPECTIVE
> On a scale of 1 to 10, with 10 representing the worst possible disaster and with 1 standing for a mere blemish, rate the particular event that is upsetting you.

$\mathcal{D}$onna's wedding day was running smoothly until it came
time for the family toasts. As expected, Marty's brother was first.
With a few hysterically funny remarks about his and Marty's adolescent exploits, he welcomed Donna into the family. But then her
father stood up and in a drone began recounting how his family
had emigrated from Russia and how they had overcome all sorts of
adversities, on and on and on for fifteen long minutes.

Donna's father rebuffed his wife's attempts to stop him.
Donna, whose face turned red with embarrassment, was growing

increasingly impatient with this man who was ruining her wedding day. She knew that there was no way to stop her pontificating father's sideshow.

Fortunately, Donna had made up a list of worst case scenarios prior to her wedding day, and tops on her list was the probability that her father might do something weird. Helplessly standing by, still listening to her father's dull monologue, Donna considered this situation on a scale of 1 to 10. She decided that things could have been worse, something could have happened before the ceremony. And the present catastrophe was only a 7—after all, how long could a toast last?

What finally saved the day was Marty's father, who firmly took the annoying man's arm and loudly said to him, "Let's go out for a breath of air." Off they went, much to everyone's relief.

For Irene it was a little more complex because of her fantasized expectations.

*F*rom the moment the guests arrived until the second they left, Irene was very disappointed with her wedding. She agonized over the thought that the photographer's flash was too bright, the flowers too ordinary, the room too small, the videographer too pushy, her grandmother too overbearing, the chicken too rubbery, the band leader too obnoxious, the cake too sickeningly sweet, and on and on. With Irene virtually in tears, her new husband, George, reassured her that everything was going just fine and encouraged her to relax and have some fun. During the good-byes, the guests warmly complimented Irene, George, and their families on a lovely affair.

A devastated and still tearful Irene went with George to Aruba, where he prohibited her from dwelling on the imperfections of their wedding day. When they returned from their recuperative two-week trip, their wedding video awaited them in the mailbox. Expecting to relive the trauma, Irene sat down with George to watch. What she saw was a lovely party in which family and friends danced, ate and drank heartily, spoke fondly of the newlyweds to the camera, and genuinely had a grand old time. Was this really her wedding day or had there been a mix-up?

Irene expected her wedding day to be complete perfection—and those unrealistic expectations over-shadowed the joy of her union to George. She cheated

PAM'S POTENTIAL
CRISIS LIST

- Mom and Dad will
  have an argument in
  front of everyone.

- My matron of honor
  will go into premature
  labor.

- The band leader will
  quit in the middle of
  the party because my
  mother-in-law will
  badger him about the
  music being too loud.

(continues)

herself out of what could have been one of the happiest days of her life.

In addition to having realistic expectations, another way to ensure that you enjoy your wedding day is to delegate a troubleshooter for the day. Select your brother, sister, or a friend—someone with a calm disposition, please. This way, your troubleshooter can quietly handle problems for you. Guests tend to watch the bride and groom like hawks, and the last thing you need is to be seen yelling at the caterer.

If things get too intense, grab your partner and a glass of champagne, and step into a quiet room for a few moments. This space you grant yourself generally works wonders. In fact, many brides and grooms take fifteen minutes to a half hour after the ceremony to be alone. They reflect on their new status, calm each other down, and simply appreciate and focus on the first few moments of matrimony.

Most importantly, however, you will be able to relax and enjoy this special celebration if you acknowledge that problems may arise, and if you identify the most likely predicaments in advance. I have heard of only a few weddings that had no flaws—be prepared for them. I usually advise my clients to make a list of all the potential hazards that could occur on their wedding day. Pam felt much better when she came up with a crisis list about a week before her gala. None of Pam's fears materialized. The wedding went off without any major impediment and she had a wonderful time because she was ready for anything.

CALMING YOURSELF

Some simple relaxation techniques can also assist you in getting through this day. If you try them out in advance you will know exactly how to create a tranquil space for yourself. Most brides find that the hardest part is waiting for the ceremony to begin. Once it does, the wedding seems to unfold naturally—like a tightly choreographed production in which everyone knows their roles. Soon you will feel yourself begin to relax, have fun, and be happy. And then it will be two o'clock in the morning and you will wonder what happened to the time.

Share the Quick Fix Relaxation Recipes with your groom, parents, siblings, and others in the wedding party. You are not the only one who is nervous! Moms, dads, siblings, grandparents, best men, maids of honor, and even friends assigned to read verses or play musical instruments can also suffer butterflies in the stomach. Here is how one nervous bride coped on her wedding day.

- My sister's baby will cry during the ceremony.
- My brother and his wife will be late for the ceremony.
- My brother will get drunk and make a spectacle of himself.
- My stepmother will feel insulted about something.
- The caterer will forget to prepare fish for my kosher relatives.
- The rabbi will step on the minister's toes.

QUICK FIX
RELAXATION RECIPES

Deep Breathing: Inhale to the count of five; hold your breath to the count of five; exhale to the count of five. Repeat twenty times. You can do this one anywhere—in the bathroom, car, even while with other people—sitting or standing.

Three, Two, One: Find a quiet place to sit with your eyes open or closed. (Try the toilet stall if you are desperate.) Focus on three things that you see, three things that you hear, and three things that you physically feel. Then do the same with two and with one. Example using one: I see the plant

(continues)

*J*oan was known to her friends and family as a jittery, high-strung woman. Everyone was anticipating that she would be a bundle of nerves at her wedding. With this in mind, extreme precautions were taken by the groom, Charley, and his sensible brother, Stuart, to prevent Joan from tripping down steps, dropping Charley's ring, or saying more than a few words during the ceremony. And indeed, on the morning of the wedding, Joan was in a complete nervous tizzy.

At the chapel she found that she had forgotten her white satin shoes along with all the make-up she had lovingly color-tested and purchased over the last month. Somehow Joan had the presence of mind to ask everyone to leave her alone in the bridal room after she made this discovery. She then took ten minutes to sit in front of the mirror where she told herself, "Joan, you must get a grip. Everything will be okay. Breathe deeply, relax, and smile. The only thing that's important today is that Charley and I are getting married. Breathe . . ."

When the bridal party walked down the aisle at noon sharp, a radiant Joan was as cool as a cucumber in her borrowed make-up and heels. It was the groom's brother Stuart who nervously took a wrong turn and ended up in the pianist's lap.

Try not to worry too much about being nervous. Even if you are jittery, hardly anyone will notice or care. Happily, it is not unusual for a serene calm to settle on the bride as she takes her first steps to Mendelssohn's refrain. It is as if your inner self decides that after all your hard work and worrying you deserve to relax and enjoy your moment in the sun.

Did you know that everything you say on this hallowed day (be it good or bad) has special meaning? So compliment your partner and reaffirm your love to him privately as well as publicly. (One couple I know ran into the bridal room immediately after the ceremony to have their first physical encounter as husband and wife. They returned to the party with even bigger smiles than when walking back up the aisle.) Take a moment to thank your parents for all they have done, and say a few kind words to your siblings, stepparents, and grandparents.

It sounds corny, but you and your partner are like angels on this day—you have the power to fulfill wishes and spread happiness. If you tell your dad you love him today, I guarantee he will remember the moment and find himself smiling even as the pain of paying the bills for the wedding lingers. If you give a little attention to your mother-in-law, your new friendship will be forged in affection. If you ask your Uncle Julius to dance with you, you just might turn around a long-standing family feud and heal his rift with your father. And if you tell your mother how great a friend and parent she has been, she may feel like her heart is exploding with joy.

across the room. I hear the music from the radio. I feel my hands shaking.

Mantra: This ancient Zen method is based on choosing a word or phrase and repeating it to yourself over and over at least twenty times. Make up your own or choose one of these reliable mantras: *ohm, relax,* or *easy does it.*

Short-cut Progressive Relaxation: Simply by attending to your body you will feel an increase in your level of relaxation. Take a comfortable position sitting or lying down, with your eyes closed. Progressively let your focus travel through your body starting with your feet, all the way up to the top of your head.

THE HONEYMOON

After all the hard work and tension of the wedding, the honeymoon offers a wonderful decompression period for the bride and groom. In most relationships, the groom handles the majority of the honeymoon planning since the bride is often more involved in designing the wedding itself. These days, couples might put off their honeymoon vacation for a week, a month, or more after the wedding in order to accommodate busy schedules.

No matter when or where it occurs, the honeymoon is a time for you to get back to the reasons you married in the first place. In all likelihood, the two of you will be isolated, leaving you plenty of time to unwind, enjoy each other's company, and think about a joyful future together.

That's the good news. There is also the other side of the honeymoon, which few marriage manuals talk about—dealing with the stress of waking up the day after your wedding ceremony to find that the man you married is not the person you thought you married. There is an adage in family therapy circles that the morning after the ceremony you awaken lying next to *thirteen* other people: your spouse, his parents, his grandparents, your parents and your grandparents.

What that means is that who you are as a person and spouse is a function of what your parents and their parents were like. Each of us tends to duplicate our own parents' and grandparents' marriages, as well as our relationship with them. You are a composite of all these relationships—a product of family patterns—yet this does not emerge until after the wedding vows have been made. In order to succeed—matrimonially speaking—your mission is to sift through all the positive and negative learning from your family of origin. Keep what is useful and discard what is detrimental.

Graduating from girlfriend to wife is enormously significant. In all cultures, including ours, the essence of the marriage ritual involves the transition from childhood to adulthood. With that passage comes innumerable new roles—different ways of behaving, additional functions, unaccustomed chores, fresh responsibilities, almost a new "you." The most significant difference is the change in your primary loyalty from your parents to your new husband.

The impact of all this movement is experienced differently by each of us. Some people move easily down the corridor of transition, while others stumbled awkwardly along the passageway from singlehood to married status. Brenda woke up sobbing the day after her wedding because she missed her mother; Kathryn, who had gone to the altar shaking and crying, felt like she really belonged to someone for the first time in her life after she said "I do." You, too, will ultimately find your own style of adjustment and grow with it.

During the first few days of the honeymoon you are on a high from the wedding, you have ample topics for conversation, and the vacation is fun. But then what? After months of frenetic wedding planning activity and communication you suddenly realize you are now alone together—for the rest of your lives—with nothing specific to do and without the usual wedding subjects to talk about. All your energy for the last six months or longer has been funneled into preparing for the wedding day, not for the marriage.

The honeymoon is more than a respite from real life. It is the period during which you will discover what your roles with each other will be, how to mesh these new roles, and how to tailor these roles to your own needs. That is the whole point of this ritual. In days of old, a honeymoon was sometimes the first real chance a couple had to get to know one another. Remember Maria and Captain Von Trapp's wedding trip, which took an entire summer? Although working couples today have fewer vacation days to devote to their honeymoon, they must still use this time wisely to rekindle their connection and enjoy each other's company.

NEWLYWEDS

It may not have seemed so, but before you got married you were on your best behavior and so was your husband. You held back on an unconscious level as a protective mechanism—this is natural. Now that you have legalized your relationship and are secure in your roles you will notice a gradual shift. While still maintaining each of your individual characteristics you will also gradually combine the two separate people you are into a new entity. You have a lot to learn and the road to enlightenment is peppered with some discomfort. Let's examine the first few months of marriage to ensure that you start out on the right foot.

FINDING YOUR BALANCE

The days, weeks, and months following the excitement of the wedding and honeymoon can be strange and

I was surprised how differently I felt toward Ron. For me it didn't occur the next day, but rather slowly over time it began to feel like we were family and were responsible to as well as for each other. I love him more now then I ever thought possible, and I feel strangely more secure and connected to him . . . nice, relaxed, at home kind of feeling. We should have married sooner.
LAURIE COLWIN

awkward for new husbands and wives. They must find a new balance and adjust to living as a couple. You tend to experience your spouse quite differently than you did when he was your boyfriend or your fiancé. For most couples, whether or not they have lived together prior to marrying, this adjustment period has a little bit of everything: some friction, some fun, and lots of joy. Let's face it, the romance between newlyweds, though still going strong, is less frenetic than before you had that wedding ring on your finger.

Only one month after their honeymoon, Tim and Julie came to my office concerned that they had made a mistake getting married. Fortunately, they quickly learned that their love for each other was still intact but that they urgently required some basic skills in learning to become a couple.

During an early session Tim asserted, "I work very hard and the last thing I need is to have problems with Julie when I get home. That is not what I got married for."

Julie was equally upset when she said, "I look forward to seeing Tim in the evening, but then all we do is get into struggles with one another. I feel like my life with my parents is being relived. I thought Tim was kind and loving, and all I get from him is criticism."

Julie and Tim needed to face facts. Marriage requires at least as much effort as a job or career. Getting to the altar is only the first part of the process. Once you return from the honeymoon both of you must be willing to work out a variety of what can sometimes be unpleasant issues. Like many men, Tim's expectations were unrealistic. Julie was right on target when she identified her new marital dance as a repetition of a familiar pattern from her family of origin. It took a true sense of commitment and a willingness to accept the initial discomfort that this change in status required. With each of them taking responsibility for some of their problems, things improved for Julie and Tim.

Chances are you and your new husband, like Julie and Tim, will also face some struggles that are the hallmark of the first few months of marriage. This period is an adjustment phase that cannot be avoided.

*J*ane Louise inwardly swooned. What an odd thing it was to have a husband. This person who was almost like a household object—a pillow or a lamp—who transformed you from a single entity into a unit, whose breathing at night was as reassuring as a clock, to whom you could, of an evening, pay almost no attention at all, and who in one minute, with one look, could turn into what a husband in actuality was: a sexual being. (From Laurie Colwin's *A Big Storm Knocked It Over.*)

Jane Louise, a fictional character, experienced what many brides talk about. She felt hysterical about being married forever and didn't really feel like herself, while she also experienced a "nuptial radiance."

*T*heir Marriage (Jane Louise further mused). It was like a museum stuffed with breakfast conversations, fights about where the extra key had been put, dinners eaten, movies viewed, showers taken together, plans made. In sickness and in health, and in confusion.

How do you deal with the implications of these transformations? Let me introduce you to the concept of building a "white picket fence" that encloses you and your spouse. This psychological boundary will hold and protect you, creating a safe emotional space for your new family—consisting of you and your husband.

The "white picket fence" is a metaphor I devised that symbolizes the boundary surrounding your magnificent alliance with your love partner. This healthy mutual commitment becomes more significant than your

other relationships, yet should not replace loving attach-
ments with family and friends. You each become more
than what you formerly were, a unit that enhances your
individual best and whose importance transcends all
other connections. As a married couple, your lives are
intrinsically tied to one another—everything that affects
one in turn alters the other. You become a "we" while
still maintaining your identity as a separate "I."

Your relationship is a precious, delicate flower that
deserves to be protected and nurtured. Toward that end
you need to construct some appropriate boundaries
dividing your tender love from the rest of the world—
including your original and extended family. Imagine a
friendly border, a fence with lots of spaces to see
through to the other side. It has a little gate that can be
closed and locked or that can be opened for traffic to
and from the outside world.

Now that you have returned from your honeymoon,
the pink haze that has enveloped you since your wedding day has lifted, and you can get a genuine view of
your new husband. Over time you cannot help but
notice certain annoying or disturbing characteristics. He
changes tables at least twice after the waiter has seated
you and you are worried about getting a reservation
again in your favorite restaurant, or he embarrasses you

with your friends when he insists on dividing the check according to what everyone ordered. Somehow you failed to observe these annoying traits during the excitement of the courtship.

Differences between you surface. That is natural; it happens to everyone and cannot be avoided. Since we each see the world from inside our own heads, having been reared in different families and having assembled different habits, we each have a unique outlook. So during this second phase of your relationship, the "adjustment phase," thousands of new rules must be instituted to smooth out the rough edges of your differences—some are implicit while others must be negotiated.

Which way do you drape the toilet paper—with the paper coming from the top or the bottom? Do you drink out of the same bathroom cup? Which way do you fold the towels? How do you make up the bed—tuck in the bottom or not? Do you sleep with the windows open, the heat on or off, a down comforter or a woolen blanket? Can you leave clothes on the chair until morning or must they be hung immediately? Do dishes get washed at once or can they pile up? Do you buy white bread or rye, store-bought or bakery? Who empties the dishwasher? When I cook, do you clean up?

Do we alternate making up the bed? Who is responsible for emptying the garbage? A thousand more details emerge that most of us do not even begin to think about until they come up as problems between us.

Then there are the basic issues that need to be negotiated. How often do you visit your parents? Do they get a key to your home? Choices about religion and religious rituals must be made. Financial decisions have to be addressed. Do you get a joint account or remain fiscally separate? What are the ramifications of each position? Do you give money to charity? Do you give money to your mother? Do you spend on theater tickets? You have to make decisions about vacations, when and whether to have children, and how many. About chores—who plans dinner, who shops, and where? About manners—do you take business phone calls during dinner? Do you call if you are going to be late? How often do you spend time apart—together? Other concerns that you might find challenging include changing your name, marital responsibility, communicating adult-to-adult with your parents, setting down roots, becoming part of your community, and whether to join a synagogue, church, or other religious group.

You can look at these issues in a variety of ways, no one is right or wrong—yet the "working out" process

ASSESSING MARITAL
ASSUMPTIONS
How many of your as-
sumptions about mar-
riage are rooted in what
you experienced by
watching your parents?
1. Make a list of every-
    thing you imagine
    marriage to be, posi-
    tive and negative.
2. On a separate sheet of
    paper, make a list of
    everything you liked
    and disliked about
    your parents' marriage.
3. Now return to your
    first list and make a
    check mark next to
    those characteristics
    that are common to
    the two lists.

often leads to tears, anger, and frustration. As long as you remind yourself and your partner that you love each other, you will be fine. Sometimes you give in, sometimes you give up, and sometimes you compromise. That is all there is.

Which brings us to the question: What has been altered in your relationship? Many people expect an idealized married life. The house will always be spotless, you and your spouse will arrive home from work at six o'clock sharp each evening, whereupon you will enjoy stimulating conversation over a candlelit dinner at the dining room table. Neighbors will stop by for coffee while you and your spouse take turns washing and drying dishes and carefully attending to each other. Or perhaps your vision includes being taken care of by your spouse, having him cater to you. But is this possible? Most of us have a truckload of marital expectations of which we are not even consciously aware.

The exercise in Assessing Marital Assumptions illuminates those tricky unrealistic little expectations that warp our view of what marriage should be. What is realistic to expect in terms of how a healthy marriage functions? In a successful marriage an interdependency develops between you and your husband—a healthy balance of independence and dependence.

The diagram below illustrates how a healthy relationship operates when there is interdependence—this term describes a balanced relationship that combines a healthy independence and dependence. Each member of the couple is responsible to and for him- or herself as well as to and for their relationship. She takes care of #1 (herself) and #3 (their marriage) and he takes care of #2 (himself) and #3 (their marriage). In this way no one is overloaded, both get taken care of, and two people are nurturing and taking care of the relationship. There is a separation, a boundary around each individ-

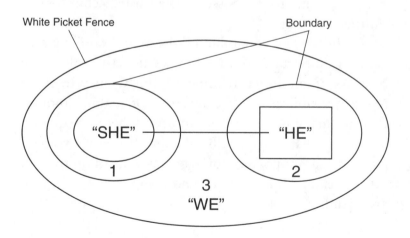

(continues)

SPRUCING UP AFTER THE WEDDING

- Think of your honeymoon as a bridge between your single and married status.
- Do not use your wedding gifts until after the ceremony.
- Introduce something new into the bedroom that did not exist prior to the wedding—mirrors, negligees, etc.—be creative.
- Address each other as Mr. and Mrs.
- Make an effort to alter some habits or routines. For example, institute new seating arrangements at the

ual so that personal development can continue. And there is the "white picket fence," which is the boundary that protects the love between you.

What can we reasonably look forward to in an intimate relationship after the wedding? Certainly we cannot expect that all of our needs will be met, that all of our problems will be solved, or that all of our dreams will come true. Unlike the prince and princess of fairy tales, we will not live happily forever after—life has a funny way of providing us with plenty of hard times. But neither are we doomed to unrelieved misery. What we can and should anticipate encountering in our relationships are healing attitudes that provide salve for our pain, solace for our losses, and a trusty anchor for our shifting fortunes.

In this day of economic hardship and family struggles, it is important for men to take an active role in the business of emotional relating and for women to share the responsibilities in the business of making money. Real intimacy is fostered in an atmosphere of equality and fairness. It cannot fully actualize between two people of disparate power. You have just signed on to each other's team. Make it work and always remember you are friends.

ABOUT PRIOR COHABITATION

If you and your new husband lived together before marriage then you had lots of company—many other like-minded couples have shared their lives even before their wedding. For you this aspect of matrimony may not feel very different. Living together was a realistic way to see if you were truly compatible, right down to whether you left the toothpaste cap off. Living with someone you love is both fun and difficult—before the wedding and after.

Sometimes people experience an anticlimax in their transition from "living together" to "married." You are now each other's family and your lives are intrinsically merged in the natural pairing system that our civilization calls "marriage." You think to yourself, shouldn't there be more of a special change? Shouldn't we feel dramatically different now that we are wed? Sprucing Up After the Wedding provides some tips you can follow to make your living arrangements feel special after the wedding.

The subtle impact of an increased commitment emerges with marriage. Some couples who have cohabited for a number of years find their relationship so drastically changed that the old rules are no longer valid. Lisa and Matthew, who had been living together

dinner table or change sides in bed.

- When introducing each other to others, be sure to say, "This is my husband, (his name)."
- Arrange one evening a week as "date night," and do something special alone together. Do not let anyone or anything interfere with that night.
- Be sure to spend one night a week away from each other. In this way you will each have interesting separate experiences that will enrich you individually, and your marriage, when you talk about them together.

for nine years, ran into trouble within six short months of getting married. What happened?

Matthew was a confirmed bachelor, who did not want to get married and made no bones about it. When Lisa agreed to living together with no strings, Matthew jumped at the chance. However, when Lisa reached her thirtieth birthday she was no longer satisfied with their undefined arrangement. Rather than lose her, Matthew reluctantly agreed to get married.

To Matthew, it seemed as if Lisa changed overnight from the exciting woman he had been in love with to a boring wife. Suddenly he felt strangled, scared, and uneasy. Neither of them understood the change in his attitude toward her, and Matthew disappeared into despair.

Lisa convinced her new husband to consult a marriage and family therapist and together they explored what the obstructions were to their happiness.

Matthew and Lisa were unprepared for the changes once they became legally linked. Becoming a wife stimulated Lisa's maternal instincts, which in turn nearly drove Matthew out the marital door. He wanted his lover, not his mother. He wanted his freedom, not a warden. They were able to save their psyches and their relationship by openly telling each other what they felt and wanted.

By becoming completely honest with one another, Lisa and Matthew created a viable marriage that worked for both of them. Lisa recognized the necessity of maintaining her role as a lover and stifled her motherly ways toward her husband. Matthew learned that he had new responsibilities as a husband that did not necessarily have to mimic his own father's unhappy sublimation in his marriage to Matthew's overbearing mother.

How do you prevent your long love affair from turning into an episode from *Divorce Court*? Listening to each other without getting defensive can be the greatest savior. The transition from cohabitation to marriage can prove difficult. But when people are willing to trust the same instincts that brought them together, they can overcome the uncertainties that follow the ceremony.

Sharing your living space with your one true love is quite different from what you initially imagined. Theoretically, you expected to play house and have lots of sex and someone to cuddle with. But the realities of this step are often underestimated and can have devastating emotional repercussions. Cohabitation leads to closeness, yet the everyday aspects of living together can also feel monotonous after a time. Marriage, the legal knot that transformed you into a family, can encourage you to make things work even when it is not easy.

On the other hand, people who marry without ever having lived with a lover have their share of domestic difficulties as well. If you have only experienced adult life as a solo pilot you have missed the opportunity to learn how to share. In circumstances where separate households were maintained before marriage, it is easier for couples to hide (usually unconsciously) aspects of their true nature from each other in an effort to preserve a peaceful relationship. (Even while cohabiting people tend to be on "better" behavior than when they actually get married.)

These artificial veils are quite impossible *and* undesirable when you are married. Undesirable because your marriage will prosper *only* when your honest and real self can connect with your partner's. Marriage seems to automatically remove the last obstacles to being your real self. But do not let that scare you too much. There is a great deal of ground you must cover as a married twosome that will create a powerful bond between you. This bond will promote genuine communication and growth—for you as an individual as well as for your relationship.

Whether you lived together before your engagement, only after the date had been set, or after you returned from the honeymoon, the real challenge is keeping your relationship happy, healthy, interesting, and erotic for the rest of your lives.

MARITAL RESPONSIBILITIES

As married adults, you have a responsibility to be mutually accountable. You ought to keep him posted, informing him about your schedule, your general whereabouts, and your future plans, and he should do the same for you. Accountability also includes consulting your partner on major decisions, purchases, and objectives. This is common marital courtesy. Yet for newly married folks this type of accountability may feel like an intrusion or a loss of freedom. Where does appropriate accountability end and subjugation begin?

How do you overcome feelings of resentment regarding this matter? A useful rule of thumb is this: You have the freedom to create a marriage that is true to your and your partner's needs. Forget what other people do or what other people think is right. By using the formula in Creating Your Own Unique Marriage, you can take your own and your husband's special individuality into account.

The ultimate objective of building accountability and responsibility into your marriage is the process of making

CREATING YOUR OWN UNIQUE MARRIAGE

- Listen to your own feelings first; what kind of marriage do you want?
- Then listen to your husband describe his feelings, thoughts, and needs.
- Like most things, you will find the solution through open, honest communication with him. Perhaps he is imposing restrictions

(continues)

a home. Creating a space that is expressive of your legal link includes a conscious shift in focus. Your home is where you reside with your partner. Your parents' home is no longer yours, it is theirs. Your task is to change your apartment or house into a real home for you and your spouse. This will necessitate decorating it together with your spouse, not with your mother or sister.

Like the children that they recently were (at least emotionally), newly married couples sometimes fight about the silliest things. One of my favorite examples is wedding thank-you notes. Nearly every couple I know has at one time or another squabbled over this mundane issue. Most brides complain that they are getting stuck doing too many of them. What's really going on?

In cases like this, it is not really the thank-yous that you are arguing about, but the nitty-gritty task of learning to cooperate as newlyweds. Dividing chores and deciding priorities often requires undertaking unpleasant adult responsibilities, which include socializing with your families, taking out the garbage, attending funerals, getting the car inspected, remembering birthdays, paying bills on time, and more. Gone are the days when Mom could sign your name to a greeting card for Grandma or write a note for you if you did not feel well enough to go to school. These humdrum adult responsibilities are enough to make anyone cranky. Try your best to divide burdens with your partner equally and according to your strengths.

Dealing with the practical aspects of adulthood is tricky. I know you think you have been an adult for some time now. But as a single person you may not have taken on the myriad of adult social tasks required by your social and family structure. Perhaps you have avoided this responsibility, or maybe you have been assuming it and it is your husband who is a novice in this field. Regardless, marriage changes you into a woman with the full credentials of a grown-up, including the responsibility of considering your husband in your decisions.

RESOLVING LEFTOVER WEDDING CONFLICTS

Chances are excellent that you have already laughed off the calamities that occurred at the wedding. Your anger over Mom's annoying interference is a faint memory. From time to time, however, a serious offense committed by a family member creates a rift that is not easily forgotten. Supposing the very worst happened, and someone in your immediate family did something so appalling at your wedding that you simply cannot forgive them.

on your time and privacy. On the other hand, perhaps you are just unaccustomed to being part of a married team. As the comedian Jerry Seinfeld said in his delightful book, *Seinlanguage,* "When you are single you can be a dictator over yourself, but when you're in a relationship everything has to be decided by committee." Whatever the problem, get to the bottom of it before it erupts.

The act itself was probably not out of character for this person. The stress of weddings can bring out the worst in some people and the best in others.

*E*verything had been in place for months. All family members were apprised of their roles for the wedding ceremony. Yet the night before Amanda and Rod were to get married turned into a nightmare. Rod's stepmother was determined to walk down the aisle with her husband despite the young couple's prior decision to limit the wedding party to their biological parents. Unfortunately, Rod's father lost sight of propriety and brought his son to tears as he verbally abused him—an old habit that Rod had not experienced since childhood.

A state of warfare ensued for the next twenty-four hours between Amanda, Rod, his father, and his stepmother. To keep up the facade of harmony at his wedding Rod capitulated—pressuring his bride to include his stepmother. The young couple was tied up in knots when they finally tied the knot. Amanda swore that she would never forgive her father-in-law.

It is not unusual for dysfunctional family dynamics to get played out during critical family events. Let's suppose that a particular occurrence hindered your ability to enjoy your wedding day. Let's further suppose that your new spouse was also affected by the family member's inappropriate behavior. Somehow you got through your wedding day. You had a few drinks; you saw that your new husband was beaming and seemed to have gotten over the crisis. Yet, weeks later you still have a heaviness in your heart. Perhaps your new spouse is still upset with your relative's behavior. You may not even be on speaking terms with the culprit or culprits. The wedding is far behind you, but the pall hangs on.

The emotional health of your marriage depends on settling ill feelings toward members of the immediate family on either side, especially if there has been a break in the relationship as a consequence of the wedding problem. Talking things out at the earliest opportunity is key. The script in Repairing Family Harmony can be helpful in structuring such a conversation.

If you expect that the culprits will admit complete blame and beg forgiveness, forget about it. The best you can hope for is that you will have successfully communicated how you experienced the incident. If you also have a sense that you were heard and understood, then you are really doing well. An apology would be a windfall. On the other hand, you may learn something new from your relative, which could alleviate your hurt feelings and change your thinking. If the meeting is a complete

REPAIRING FAMILY
HARMONY

1. Wait only as long as
   you need to pacify
   your sensitive feelings.
2. Choose a neutral
   place for you and
   your spouse to meet
   with the relative(s).
3. Make your goals
   explicit when you
   invite them to join a
   conversation designed
   to work things out.
4. The partner whose
   relative is being
   addressed should
   lead the discussion.
5. Begin by asking for
   their attention without
   interruption—promis-
   ing their turn to speak.
6. Describe how you
   experienced the situa-
   tion, making sure to
   stick to "I" language.

(continues)

disaster, leave yourself open to future opportunities to iron out differences.

Regardless of the ill treatment you received at the time of your wedding, I urge you not to even consider ending your relationship with a member of your or your spouse's family of origin. Marriage and family therapists unanimously agree that cutting off a family member is never a viable solution because it cuts deeply into your psychological essence! Feelings of unresolved anger poison your ability to love freely and connect genuinely with others. There is never sufficient reason to completely end your relationship with a member of your family of origin.

Although you cannot always have the sort of relationship you would prefer, you need to solve the differences between you to the best of your ability. Eventually, it would benefit you to come to terms with every member of your families in order to have emotionally healthy relationships with your spouse and future children.

Why? Because there is a tendency to repeat dysfunctional patterns of interaction from one generation to the next through a process called transference. When your relationships with mother, father and siblings are relatively free of conflict and stress—a cut-off by definition implies conflict—you stand a better chance of channeling loving energy within your immediate realm.

The key is to understand what motivates each family member and to accept each of them with their limitations. If you can be sympathetic to their inadequacies it will be easier to forgive them. Then you can determine what kind of connection is possible with them considering their shortcomings. Perhaps your relationship can only be a distant one, but there should be some semblance of a "relationship" that you can manage.

*J*une was devastated by her father's behavior at her wedding. He got drunk, was lewd and insulting to some of the guests, and made a general spectacle out of himself. Prior to that day, June had not fully faced her father's problem with alcohol. Afterwards, she lost all feelings of affection for this man. She tried many times to heal the breach between them, but was repeatedly stymied in her efforts by his vehement system of denial. She came to realize that her father had a serious illness and deep emotional problems, and that she could never change him. Determined to act in a psychologically healthy fashion, she decided it would be sufficient to stay connected with him for the present time through abbreviated monthly telephone calls and infrequent family gatherings.

7. Now stop and listen to their point of view. Do not interrupt.

8. Repeat step 5 and respond by validating their feelings. For example, "I can understand that you may have felt this way," or "So your feelings were hurt, too."

9. Ask if they understand your position and then listen.

10. If at anytime the discussion dissolves into a screaming match, it is imperative for you to resist going on. Call a halt and try again another day. (When the clouds clear, be sure to examine how your own input, or your spouse's, may have exacerbated things.)

A DELICIOUS RECIPE
FOR MARITAL BLISS
Take a generous helping
    of *love;*
Blend together a healthy
    measure of *fairness*
    and *cooperation;*
Mix well with a cup
    each of *compassion,*
    commitment, and
    compromise;
Gently fold in a gallon
    of *tolerance;*
Add a bucketful of
    forgiveness;
Sprinkle a heaping table-
    spoon of *humor;*
Stir in a dash of *sex* and
    a pinch of *fun;*
And do not forget to
    choose your battles.

Keep in mind that people make mistakes, albeit grand ones at times, and that a "relationship" is much more important than a fragment of behavior.

FREE TO BE MARRIED: A BLESSING

I am going to share a little secret with you. I have always wished that I could be a fairy godmother. You know, the type that can wave a magic wand and grant people their heart's true desire. In my years of experience as a marriage and family therapist, I have met hundreds of wonderful single and engaged people whose fondest wish was to become happily married. Yet again and again their wishes were not being granted.

Some had problems achieving a committed relationship. Some were ambivalent about taking the next step toward marriage. There were those who broke off their engagement due to unexpected premarital pressures on their relationship. All of these incidents were traced to effects of dysfunctional family patterns, low self-esteem, inadequate interpersonal communication skills, emotional underdevelopment, and lingering fears regarding intimacy. Eventually these people came to me looking for answers.

Each and every one of these men and women were entitled to marital happiness. I often wished that my job could be as easy as sprinkling them with pixie dust, or telling them to click their heels together three times and make a wish. The truth is that most personal obstacles that stand in one's way of finding love and a happy marriage cannot just be wished away. Many of these issues have actually been hidden for years and they cannot be remedied in the blink of an eye. These issues need to be uncovered, carefully probed, and then rearranged into new configurations that have fresh meaning and allow for new attitudes and new behavior.

I like to think that this book is the best available substitute for a magic wand. It explores and offers solutions to the many cultural and personal issues that make getting married such an emotionally complicated process. I trust that you now have the tools to survive the emotional curves thrown at you while organizing your wedding day. Most especially, I hope your newfound knowledge and skills will allay your uncertainty and boost you toward enjoying this very special time of engagement.

It is never easy to delve into issues that lie close to home. But as Dorothy from Kansas once suggested,

"The next time you go searching for your heart's desire, why not start in your own backyard?" It turns out Dorothy did not need magic, and neither do you. As the good witch explained to her, "You've had the power all along!"

And so do you. If you remain focused on achieving your goal of a joyful wedding and a successful marriage, saying "I do!" will just be the beginning of your real-life "happily (most of the time) ever after."

RECOMMENDED READING

Bach, G., and Wyden, P., *The Intimate Enemy*. Avon, 1968.

Bepko, C., and Krestan, J., *Too Good for Her Own Good*. Harper & Row, 1990.

Bok, S., *Lying*.Vintage, 1979.

Branden, N., *The Psychology of Romantic Love*. Bantam, 1985.

Cowan, P. and R., *Mixed Blessings—Overcoming Stumbling Blocks in an Interfaith Marriage*. Doubleday, 1987.

Edelman, H., *Motherless Daughters*. Addison-Wesley, 1994.

Frankl, V. E., *Man's Search for Meaning*. Simon & Schuster, 1984.

Fried, E., *The Courage to Change*. Evergreen, 1981.

Lederer, W. J., and Jackson, D., *The Mirages of Marriage*. Norton, 1968.

Lerner, H. G., *The Dance of Anger*. Harper & Row, 1985.

———, *The Dance of Intimacy*. Harper & Row, 1989.

Love, P., *Hot Monogomy*. Dutton, 1994.

McGoldrick, M., and Gerson, R., *Genograms*. Norton, 1985.

McKay, M., and Rogers, P., *When Anger Hurts*. New Harbinger, 1989.

Napier, A., and Whitaker, C., *The Family Crucible*. Harper & Row, 1978.

Paul, J., and Paul, M., *Do I Have to Give Up Me to Be Loved by You?* Compcare, 1983.

Rogers, C., *Becoming Partners*. Dell, 1972.

Rubin, L., *Intimate Strangers*. Harper & Row, 1983.

Rubin, T., *The Angry Book*. Collier Macmillan, 1969.

Singer, L., *Stages: The Crises That Shape Your Marriage*. Grosset & Dunlap, 1980

Smedes, L., *Forgive and Forget*. Harper & Row, 1984.